A MAVERICK INVESTOR'S GUIDEBOOK

Also by the author

Resources Rock

A MAVERICK INVESTOR'S GUIDEBOOK

Invest to Live, Live to Ride

MAL SPOONER

INSOMNIAC PRESS

Library and Archives Canada Cataloguing in Publication

Spooner, Malvin, 1955-
A maverick investor's guidebook / Mal Spooner.

ISBN 978-1-55483-016-9 trade paperback
ISBN 978-1-55483-037-4 ebook

1. Investments. 2. Finance, Personal. I. Title.

HG4521.S66 2011 332.6 C2011-900341-4

The publisher gratefully acknowledges the support of the Department of Canadian Heritage through
the Book Publishing Industry Development Program.

Insomniac Press
520 Princess Avenue, London, Ontario, Canada, N6B 2B8
www.insomniacpress.com

Canada

I'd like to dedicate this book to all
law enforcement officers, firefighters, and the military.
Not only do they risk their lives for us all, many are also
avid motorcycle enthusiasts.

CONTENTS

INTRODUCTION

Consider my preferred definition of *maverick* (mav-er-ik, mav-rik) (plural, mav-er-icks), as found in the *Encarta World English Dictionary*: "an independent thinker who refuses to conform to the accepted view on a subject." The term originally referred to an animal that strayed from the herd. Our instincts drive us towards the herd, believing there is safety in numbers. We are, after all, a social species. Unfortunately, a cattle drive usually leads to the wholesale slaughter of the entire herd.

My work has always been my passion, and my Harley-Davidson motorcycles and guitars are my hobbies. What do I mean by *passion?* A passion is always challenging, rather than relaxing. You can easily distinguish a passionate golfer from a hobby golfer. A passionate golfer is never satisfied. They never feel good enough. They are always challenging themselves, striving to learn more, and gradually but methodically working to get just a little better at the game. Extraneous emotions are the real handicap. Happiness, anxiety, fear, and rage, for example, only hinder success. And there is no endpoint. A game has a finish, but then another game will begin. A passion has no beginning, middle, or end.

I decided to write this guidebook while riding from my

home in Toronto, Ontario, through the United States to the west coast and back. The loud pipes, fresh air, and music help keep my head clear of the little details and petty emotions that clutter the mind, allowing me to focus on sharing with you the invaluable lessons I've learned throughout my thirty years as a money manager—one who founded, grew, and ultimately sold an investment management company.

How does this relate to investment philosophy, theory, and practice? To successfully invest your money or someone else's money, it's absolutely crucial to strip your mind and spirit of emotions but remain passionate. Since your coworkers, friends, and family are by and large incapable of investing their savings with cool indifference to feelings, you will have to become a maverick. In fact, their emotions will prove to be excellent indicators for you. A constant theme for the maverick is "do the opposite." Not just for the sake of being contrarian, but because going your own way will usually be a calculated response to an obvious opportunity that has presented itself.

I was a portfolio manager for institutional clients early in my career. This means I managed money for pension funds, endowment, and mutual funds, and never had to actually communicate with real people. One day out of the blue, a mushroom farmer, who had his own little airplane, flew into the big city looking for a "professional" to manage his money. It wasn't a trivial sum—something like a couple of million dollars—but I was used to portfolios that were bigger by one or more zeros. I took a shining to him, however, and agreed to take on the assignment.

Do you remember the crash of '87, Black Monday? Well, shortly after October of 1987, Mushroom Man contacted me, and his friendly demeanour was all but gone. He asked for a meeting immediately. I obliged, and when we met, he indicated he was disappointed with his investment performance and would like to discontinue the arrangement. I explained to him that despite the carnage that took place in all markets, he was actually "in the money" by something like 8%—nothing to jump up and down about, perhaps, but way better than a kick in the head. This was also much superior to what my institutional clients suffered.

All my efforts to demonstrate that $X + 8% means you actually *made* money just weren't sinking in. He wouldn't listen or simply didn't *believe* me. Apparently, his accountant had looked at the cost of several stocks (i.e. the prices paid for the stocks) held in the portfolio. The accountant concluded that I was doing a lousy job for Mushroom Man because the prices paid were higher than the current market prices. Keep in mind that virtually everyone else had just watched their entire savings plummet by 30% or more in a few short months and were helpless to do anything about it. It happened so fast that the stock exchanges couldn't keep up with the hysterical selling, and there were no buyers to be had anyway.

Question: How do you measure success?

I felt proud about preserving Mushroom Man's money, although admittedly it wasn't because I was brilliant. I'm not shy to admit that I never saw Black Monday coming and was just lucky to have picked a few good stocks for him. The maverick in me said, "Be patient and these prices will improve again once the panic subsides." More important, I had no intention of resting on my laurels and was already looking for superior stocks (better in terms of their potential to appreciate from depressed levels) that I could use to replace the ones held in the portfolio.

If success is measured by client satisfaction, I admit I failed miserably. No facts were going to change his mind. Even though his accountant didn't seem to understand how to measure a rate of return (it's harder to calculate than most think it is), the accountant's assessment was more in tune with the prevailing bearish herd mentality prevalent at that time.

Answer: There is no single measure of success!

Neither my pride nor my client's distress had anything to do with success or failure. He gave me every indication that he could tolerate risk so long as his capital grew over time. If this indeed was his goal, then allowing himself to be infected by a sudden deterioration in the mood of the masses created a failure in the overall plan. If he'd left everything alone, or elected to invest more while markets were cheap, then the inevitable rebound in markets—and yes it's always inevitable (more about this later)—would have advanced his mission to become just a bit wealthier. Emotion got in the way. The whole exercise was a hobby for him, and since it no longer made him happy, he quit. You cannot, however, just quit a passion.

I am not personally wealthy by any stretch of the imagination, unlike some of the "gurus" who made fortunes and proceeded to publish memoirs or how-to books to make themselves even more money. I've mentioned there is no single measure of success. For me, success has meant earning a satisfying living managing investment portfolios for others, loving my friends and family, training young traders and portfolio managers, and creating jobs for people so they too can lead satisfying lives. Real success for me is having the knowledge on my deathbed that I was always honest and fair with others.

Although I lectured a university course on introductory economics once, I am not a teacher. The purpose of this guidebook is not to teach you how to invest or to educate the reader about different types of securities and how they work. There's a plethora of those types of books out there. What those books don't teach you is how you must think in order to make successful investment decisions with your money. I have purposely avoided getting into details about formulas, research analysis, and micro- or macroeconomic theory. This is partly because it would bore me to tears, but it's mostly because none of that with help you unless you first develop a maverick approach to investing.

Part One of this guidebook is devoted to sharing with you what other investors (including myself on occasion) do wrong and what a maverick investor won't do. Take our experience and make it your experience by reading it. Part Two discusses important things a maverick investor should know before mounting up and trailblazing into the world of financial markets. With Parts One and Two in your back pocket, Part Three, understanding what a maverick investor does and why, will make a lot more sense. In Part Four, we examine how to judge your progress along the investment trail and determine what sort of market environment you are in and how to plan for the trail ahead. Part Five outlines "road stories" that may help you cope with failure and success along that trail.

Investing is like life, and life is like touring on a Harley: There's an infinite array of places to go and as many routes to choose from that will get you there. Don't let your emotions or what others think steer you from your goals.

1) Decide where you want to go.

Are you primarily interested in a flow of income? If so, how can you get the highest yield? Learn the difference between before-tax and after-tax yield. The chart below is from an old presentation of mine:

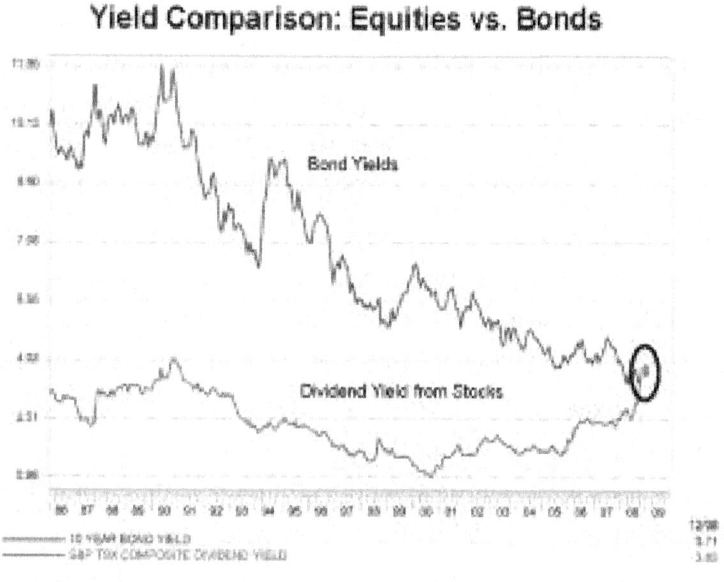

The graph illustrates that back in November 2008 the stock market (the Toronto Stock Exchange Index) had declined so much that the average dividend yield for stocks was in absolute terms as high as the yield for a 10-year

Government of Canada bond. The amount you get to keep after tax is even higher because dividends are taxed at a more favourable lower rate than interest income. If you were to screen for higher dividend yields than the average at that time and bought the stocks, you made out like a bandit. In addition to the generous dividend yield the shares paid, stock prices also recovered as they always do.

You may instead be looking for your money to grow gradually, or maybe you have a more aggressive nature and are willing to take more risk for a bigger return. Bonds occasionally grow in price more than stocks. Most people don't know this, and it's worth doing a bit of homework on your own to discover why this is true. If you invested in bonds before the bond yields began declining (see graph above), your rate of return over the period of falling yields would be far in excess of the monthly interest payments paid to you, and you would have whopping capital gains in the value, or market price, of those bonds as well.

2) Map out a way to go in order to get there.

Once you've decided where you want to go with your investments, you will want to figure out how to get there. As you can tell from the above, and as we will discuss in coming chapters, much of what you might believe or have read in the press or from others (even your financial advisor) is often a far cry from what is true.

The early chapters in this guidebook discuss what not to do. You can simply invest in a relatively diversified portfolio over a long period—a sort of buy-and-hold approach often recommended by lazy advisors—and *hope* you make a decent return. For some, hope springs eternal, but a maverick would rather understand market psychology and dynamics in order to improve the prospects for getting the most out of their money.

Some people are inclined to manage their own portfolio, buying and selling stocks or bonds or fancy options strategies, while others use mutual funds and/or hedge funds or simply work with an advisor. The approach you take will depend on your level of sophistication and interest, the time you can devote to doing your own research, and how much money you are prepared to put "at risk." The maverick mindset I hope to help you develop will make any route you choose to adopt highly successful. Later chapters will be devoted to learning how to think like an investment maverick when making important decisions like these.

3) Always be prepared to adjust your route due to obstructions and detours.

Working in the investment industry is fascinating, mostly because things change fast and furiously. Like twisting and turning down a mountain road on a motorcycle, you must learn to adapt to changing circumstances quickly. There will often be an urge to panic in light of events, but every hazard presents opportunities if you keep a level head.

While the recent financial crisis frightened the vast majority of investors away from stocks, the maverick investor would have found the high dividend yield a comfortable cushion against risk, especially with the selection of companies that remained financially strong despite the recessionary economy (Canadian bank stocks for example) or mutual funds invested in stocks paying dividends or other forms of income distribution.

4) Getting to your destination is your only measure of success.

If your expectations are ridiculous, you will never be successful. There will be obstacles, and you will make (hopefully infrequent) mistakes along the way. When you get lost on the road, you would simply stop and calmly get out a map or ask for directions. You would reorient yourself, and as long as you arrive at your destination, you're content. Would you kick yourself if you discovered some other traveller managed to get to the same destination sooner? It's remarkable how some investors feel devastated when they learn someone else is making more money in a stock or mutual fund than they are. All of a sudden, they are willing to throw caution to the wind and mimic another investor's strategy. The other investor may have just gambled and was lucky, with no other objective than to get some thrills playing the market. We will examine the difference between gambling and investing.

5) Enjoy the ride.

If you learn from the mistakes I've made or witnessed that are outlined in the following pages, then you will avoid panic and traffic jams, and the knowledge will steer your investments in the right direction. You will eventually arrive where you want to go safely and you will find the ride enjoyable.

PART ONE

WHAT A MAVERICK INVESTOR WON'T DO

CHAPTER 1

NEVER PANIC! WHAT CRISIS?

Panic is a killer. On a motorcycle, it can mean almost certain death. I recall twisting and turning down an Australian mountain road. I was having such a great time that I didn't notice that my speed was getting up there. I wasn't really thinking when my right hand applied the brake in the middle of a sharp turn. When you apply brakes in a turn on a bike, oddly enough it makes the bike go straighter. Instead of leaning into the turn more aggressively, and you can lean a motorcycle pretty low without losing control, here I was unconsciously forcing the bike to head straight towards the guardrail and a cliff. Panic could have caused a *Thelma & Louise* ending for me, but despite how fast things were happening, I did have time to a) come to my senses, b) shout, "Oh @&#%!" and c) think fast enough to let go of the brake and lean hard into the turn. All the while, my daughter was on the back, plugged into her iPod, and so was oblivious to the near disaster.

Maverick investing is understanding that panic is a sensation best controlled. Panic will rear its head on multiple occasions, but the successful investor can't let it influence judgement. It's okay to experience panic, but a maverick will fight the urge to succumb to it.

Most "hobby" investors, whether they're day trading, switching in and out of mutual funds based on the most recent performance rankings, or using an advisor for the first time, will panic during a financial crisis and it will probably be the last time they actively invest in markets.

Here is just a small sampling of the great financial panics since the turn of the twentieth century:

- Stock Market Crash of 1929 (aka the Great Crash)
- The 1973–75 recession
- The recent financial crisis of October 2007 to November 2008

A market panic occurs in a few steps:

1) Stock markets fall rapidly and unexpectedly. This is because there are suddenly far more sellers of securities than there are buyers.
2) News travels fast. Markets are actually an information industry. As stock prices decline (as well as the prices of other assets such as bonds, real estate, and commodities such as oil or copper), all sorts of investors begin to panic and try to sell their stocks and any other assets deemed to be vulnerable—and this all happens at the same time.
3) Anyone who might have been interested in buying assets is spooked by the landslide of selling and postpones any action.
4) Once the dust settles, volumes on stock exchanges and other markets dry up. Sellers realize they can't sell if there

are no buyers. Potential buyers are worried that anything they buy will devalue even more. Checkmate.

The Dow Jones Industrial Average (DJIA) is an index of thirty large publicly traded U.S. companies. It isn't very representative of the broader economy, but because it has been around a long time, it serves as a convenient measure of the overall stock market's direction. When the DJIA is climbing in value, investors are happy and making money. When its value falls, investors are losing money and miserable.

There's been much written about the Great Crash and Black Monday. As soon as the opening bell rang on Monday, October 28th, 1929, stock prices began to slide. By the end of the day, the Dow had fallen in value by a whopping 13%. Nowadays, we're more accustomed to volatility, but back then, a single-day loss of such magnitude was considered apocalyptic. So many shares changed hands that day that pro traders didn't even have time to record them all.

After that fateful day, the Dow kept falling. From its highest level in September 1929, the index declined 89% by July 1932. If my experience is any guide, the lion's share of investor money went into the market shortly before the Crash, attracted by the great returns earned "by others" over the previous few years. In other words, large numbers of novice investors were left with a paltry 10% of their original investment almost overnight and would never buy stocks again.

Suddenly between 1932 and 1933, the Dow rallied 162%. Those who did panic and sold during the dark days completely missed the inevitable rebound. It would take twenty-two years (by November of 1954) for the Dow to get back to its previous high, but it did. No, you didn't have to wait twenty-two years to make your money back. We will explore superior strategies to just buying and waiting later in the guidebook.

Beginning January 1973 until December 1974, the Dow fell 45%, anticipating a recession that lasted sixteen months. The recession technically lasted until March 1975, but by June 1975, the Dow had rallied 51% from its lowest level. Investors were still selling while it was clear that the market, which is always one step ahead of the economy still at the tail end of a recession, had already begun to rally. It may seem trite to say, "Hey, markets go down, and then up, and so on," but no matter how often it occurs, people repeatedly make the same mistakes.

I've been asked many times over the years to help calm the clients of financial advisors in group meetings or seminar formats following market meltdowns. Despite showing them the chart on the following page, as well as other similar graphs as exhibits, very few folks actually modify their behaviour. In most other life experiences, where the expression "once bitten, twice shy" applies, people do learn from their mistakes. For unknown reasons, this learning process is altogether missing when it comes to people and their money. Some people are completely disillusioned by their first experience buying high and selling low, and so they quit trying. Far too many other folks make the same mistake repeatedly. They wait until the mob is euphorically investing money, whether in stocks, bonds, real estate, mutual funds, or hedge funds, and dive in with everyone else.

If they make a little money at it, they increase their investment like inexperienced gamblers in Las Vegas. Then when the tide turns and investment losses are at their worst, these poor folks sell everything and suffer huge losses.

Crisis	Market Low	Gain on Capital Markets (5)	
		1 Year	2 Year
The Korean War	13-Jul.-50	28.80%	39.30%
Cuban Missile Crisis	23-Oct.-62	25.00%	57.30%
1969/70 Market Break	26-May-70	43.60%	53.90%
1973/74 Market Break	6-Dec.-74	42.20%	66.50%
1979/80 Oil Crisis	27-Mar.-80	27.90%	5.90%
1987 Stock Market Crash	19-Oct.-87	22.90%	54.30%
Desert Storm	11-Oct.-90	21.10%	30.20%
Average Appreciation		**30.40%**	**43.90%**

Rebounds from crises are inevitable. Despite this fact, remarkably few investors are able to either:

A) figure out in advance that when markets are strong, one ought to be selling rather than buying, or
B) learn the hard way that going with the ebb and flow of the herd is an irrational approach to investing their money and adopt a smarter approach.

Being a maverick isn't easy!

During October of 1987, my wife and I were touring around Europe. Consequently, I had no idea about the market collapse that would be labelled the "crash of '87." Upon my return to work, I was delighted to discover so many of the companies I had invested in (The Gap comes to mind as one of them) were ridiculously cheaper than when I had left for my vacation a couple of weeks earlier. The stock market seemed to me like a big warehouse sale.

Back in the office, I was diligently going over my own research and buying more of the stocks that I considered exceptional value at depressed prices. Then one afternoon, the big boss from our parent company decided to visit our offices to console the troops. After all, most portfolio managers had watched the stocks they held in portfolios get pummeled in real time. All of them were now immobilized like deer in the headlights.

When the boss came to my office, he was taken aback by my obvious jubilance. "What are you up to, Mal? How are you coping?" I responded, perhaps not wisely, that things were fantastic, and told him I was buying stocks like crazy. I later learned from my immediate supervisor that the big boss that same day suggested I should be fired immediately. Thank goodness my supervisor, who was blessed with more experience and tact than I, was a bit of a maverick himself and understood what I was doing. He stuck up for me.

Whenever you are expressing an opinion or behaving in a fashion inconsistent with a peer group or society, there will be efforts to bring you back into the fold. If you remain stubborn, expect to be ostracized. As a result, I wasn't exactly popular with my fellow employees in the ensuing months. It's a curse! When your behaviour is counter to that of the herd, your community will simply think you're daft. But if it turns out you were right and they were all wrong, you are suddenly the devil incarnate in their eyes.

Exactly one year later, the same big boss congratulated

me on the outstanding investment performance of the funds I was managing and proceeded to assign me a couple hundred million dollars with instructions to go ahead and invest the money "my" way. There's the rub: By doing what I knew to be the smart thing to do, I may have been unemployed by the time any good came of it.

There are at least two lessons I took away from this:

1) Maverick investing works.
2) Don't be too vocal about what it is you're doing.

Common sense dictates that the first lesson is true, and we'll be exploring numerous examples on various levels in future chapters, including identifying industry trends, picking mutual funds, and stock selection.

The second lesson is simply an admission that people are extremely sensitive to anything you might say or do that confirms they are stupid.

During the more recent financial crises but *after* the markets declined, investors transferred record amounts of their savings out of stocks, bonds, and other assets into short-term government treasuries, GICs (guaranteed investment certificates offered by banks and other financial institutions), and money market funds that effectively were paying a zero rate of interest. In retrospect, these investors now know they acted irrationally and are reluctant to even talk about it. Many rationalize their panic by insisting that the *crisis* is not yet over. Rather than admit they've forgone a huge rebound in market valuations during 2009 and some of 2010, and developing some forward-thinking tactics as a maverick investor would do, they sit on their laurels.

Financial Crisis? What Crisis?

I don't really mean to seem flippant. It's obvious that the crisis that stemmed from an artificially bloated U.S. housing market, and the creation of multiple billions of dollars of virtually counterfeit financial instruments on the back of it, has taken its toll on everyone in the world. Even maverick fund managers who had no exposure whatsoever to the worthless mortgage-backed paper and countless derivatives that posed as assets suffered from the fallout in global markets.

The maverick investor knows history may indeed repeat itself, but seldom does it happen immediately. Economists, investment strategists, and investment analysts have a bad habit of forecasting what has just happened—at least until things have changed, and even then, they are slow to adjust their forecasts. I know it sounds preposterous, but I base my conclusion on reading loads of crap over several decades. It was my job. These nefarious predictions always manage to find their way into the financial press and business television, and they only serve to corrupt the decisions of both innocent novice investors and professional money managers alike. I picked two headlines published on June 30, 2010, to illustrate my point.

In one newspaper, under the title "Economic crisis," I found the headline: "World recovery under threat as growth slows, stimulus wanes." On the same day in another newspaper, under the title "Recovery angst" was the similarly ominous caption: "Economic trouble is all investors see."

If you are spooked by such nonsense and inclined to adopt a wait-and-see approach before investing any of your money at all in financial markets, then give your head a shake. These headlines are gold! The maverick in you should begin to wonder: If the press is even partially representative of what economists and strategists are recommending, and if investors *all* share the same sentiments, then what happens when there's some good news? Everyone is sitting idly on the sidelines and still hasn't bought into the market, or they sold everything they held all the way down at the market bottom. An improvement in virtually anything ranging from consumer buying, corporate profitability, or, God willing, a boost in global growth will create a buying binge.

The maverick investor will want to be invested before the herd moves from bearish to bullish. Buy when things seem bleak, and on the flipside, be ready to sell when everything seems rosy. Always be thinking ahead. Hockey legend Wayne Gretzky was the undisputed maverick on skates. He would not skate to where the puck had been, or even where it was. Gretzky built a spectacular career by determining where the puck was going to be.

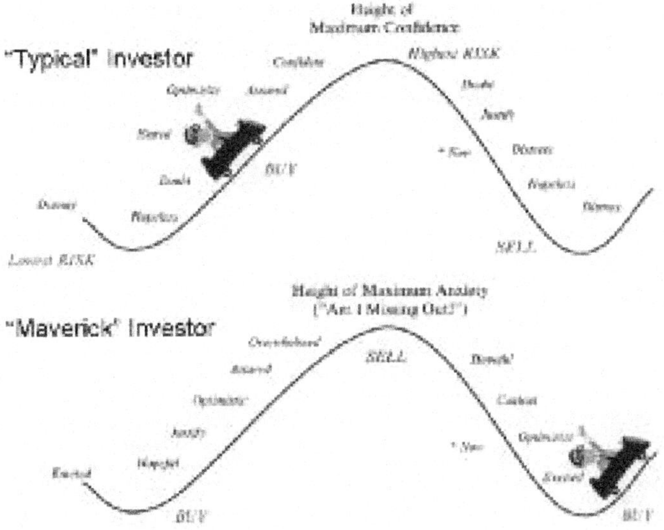

It's all about anticipating the road ahead, rather than having to react when it's too late. Heading out on a road trip involves thinking ahead. Of course you need to pack rain gear, maps, and a toothbrush, but the most important preparation is in the mind. Before even leaving the garage, you must have trained yourself to *never panic!*

CHAPTER 2

AVOID HEAVY TRAFFIC! GO AGAINST THE FLOW!

I find it remarkable that humankind will devise ingenious methods of identifying where traffic is heavy to make it easier to avoid it. Folks will spend valuable time listening to their favourite radio station for traffic updates or spend money on GPS services that identify congestion hotspots. When it comes to investing their money, however, they spend time and money looking for traffic and trying hard to squirm into the middle of it.

Becoming a maverick investor can come from reasoning, listening to advice from a more seasoned investor, or learning the hard way. In some respects, learning the hard way is the best way to learn, but it is incredibly expensive.

While I was doing my MBA, I became fascinated with markets. After all, it seemed that my graduate school background in economics taught me as much as I needed to know about fiscal and monetary policy, business cycles, supply and demand, cost curves, and the gamut. I spent many hours studying stock charts and earnings reports. I developed a simple model to screen for the best performing publicly traded stocks and inspired a group of fellow students to start an investment club. It all made so much sense to me.

All the stocks that ended up in our portfolio had stock price charts that looked like hockey sticks, and earnings that had been growing in the double digits for a few years running.

Myth: The stock price of a company goes up because the company's earnings go up!

We were students (borderline idiots) who bought into the myth that one just has to find companies with rising earnings and the stock prices or value of the business will rise too. The question we neglected to ask, indeed the most important question, was why the stock price really was rising.

They call it a stock "market" for a good reason. Like every market, there are buyers of stuff and sellers of stuff. If the price of something trading in a market is rising, it's because more people are buying than selling. You want an item bad enough? Then you have to pay a little more than a competing buyer to the guy who has the item for sale.

Back in 1973, the Yom Kippur War (when Syria and Egypt attacked Israel) ignited the Arab Oil Embargo and rising oil prices, but it was the Iranian Revolution and the Iran–Iraq War that witnessed disruptions in oil supply. Consequently, oil prices rose from $5 per barrel in 1973 to $38 by 1980. Wow!

Did I mention that our investment club was formed in 1980? We were dazzled by this past run-up in oil prices and its impact on several companies. In fact, every stock in our portfolio was invested in either oil and gas exploration companies, companies that owned gas stations, companies involved in real estate (in Calgary, Alberta, particularly), or some other business that had been benefitting from higher energy prices. Admittedly, everyone at the time believed oil prices would continue on their upward trajectory forever.

We were just joining the herd. Basically, all my brilliant modelling did was direct us right into heavy traffic. Investors of every ilk had been moving into energy stocks for a couple of years, bidding up stock prices. It was a financial traffic jam of epic proportions.

Unexpectedly, a nasty economic recession hit shortly afterward during 1981 and 1982. High oil prices and suddenly much less money in the pockets of consumers pummelled the demand for oil. Interest rates also were sky high, as President Ronald Reagan tried to combat rampant inflation. By 1986, the price of oil, despite attempts by OPEC to control production levels and stabilize prices, had sunk to about $11 per barrel. The earnings of our portfolio companies in the business of producing or selling oil, and any service companies that benefitted from the oil industry boom, all plummeted. More important, so did their stock prices until our portfolio had been reduced to rubble. All the traffic had suddenly shifted, with investors now selling the energy sector with no buyers. Investment traffic was heading in another direction, and we'd stalled.

Truth: The stock price of a company goes up because people are buying it.

Corollary 1: If the stock price has already gone up a lot, people have already bought it.

Corollary 2: If everyone already owns it, there's nobody left to buy it.

Where There's Traffic, There's Trouble

When the world's largest oil-consuming economy slumped with the price of oil along with it, all of us who had been jamming together to own energy stocks now wanted desperately to sell them and fast—especially those who had owned the stocks long enough to make a profit. Unfortunately, it's the herd selling in unison that causes stock prices to tumble even faster. It's like a financial avalanche, moving too fast for investors to get out of the way.

If all the above sounds remarkably like the message delivered in the first chapter, then you're paying attention. The global markets are the sum of the markets of different countries, which are the sum of those countries' various industries, which are the sum of corporations and ultimately individuals. In Chapter 1, the emphasis was "never panic," whereas in this chapter, the emphasis is on what things to watch for to avoid being in a panic situation in the first place.

The first leg of my road trip was from Toronto, Ontario, to Chicago, Illinois. I left on a Saturday, since my maverick instincts suggested traffic on highways and at border crossings would be less congested on the weekend. It was smooth sailing, and thank God it was because the temperature was in the mid-90s Fahrenheit (mid-30s Celsius) and there's no air conditioning on my new 2009 Harley-Davidson Electra-Glide Classic.

I sold my older touring bike since I didn't think it would be able to survive such a long trip. That bike and I travelled many miles together and it broke my heart to part with it—sort of like losing a dear friend. Stop laughing now; it really was traumatic to see someone else drive off with my memories.

When I reached the border crossing at Sarnia, Ontario, there was, of course, a lineup. It wasn't as big as would be the case on a weekday, but it was a lineup nevertheless, and a maverick deplores traffic of any sort. After all, here I was sitting in a lineup on a motor that runs at more than 250°F on a day where the outside temperature was almost 100°F. If I didn't do something, there *would* be panic.

I asked a fellow in an air-conditioned car beside me if he'd let me back into the line nearer the interrogation booth. He agreed, and I drove the bike up near the front of the line and shut off the engine, dismounted, and removed my helmet.

Suddenly, three border guards started walking towards me, hands at the ready on their firearms and with scowls on their faces.

"What are you doing?" one of them asked.

"I'm waiting. It's really hot sitting directly on an engine with two wheels, and the fellow in the car I was next to at the back said he'd let me in when he got up to the front."

"You can't do that! This is a secure area."

Another guard came out to join in the ruckus. "Is everything under control here?"

"Yes," the first guy said, and he turned to me and said, "Because you tried to avoid the line, I'm going to have to take you inside for an interview."

"If it's air conditioned, I'm okay with that," I respond happily.

"Park your bike over there, and follow me inside please."

While he and another border guard rummaged through my bike out in the scorching heat, I waited in air-conditioned comfort inside. Of course, there's not a whole lot of room to hide stuff worth smuggling on a motorcycle. I couldn't imagine what they'd be looking for. A Canadian would most likely shop south of the border and try to smuggle items back into Canada rather than the other way around. And why would I have weapons? They are more plentiful and a heck of a lot cheaper in the U.S.

I even had entertainment. A Japanese family was being interviewed next to me and couldn't speak a word of English. I witnessed homeland security hard at work. I'm still thoroughly enthralled with the border guard's efforts to communicate with the Japanese family when "my" guard returns and hands me back my passport.

"Don't try that again. Other people have to sit in their vehicles and wait. Many of those cars aren't air conditioned, so they have to suffer the heat too, you know." (But at least they have shade, don't they?)

"You better stay in the line next time, and you won't have to go through this inconvenience. After all, we don't know what you're planning when you do something like that in a secure area. It is a border crossing, damn it! You can go now."

It reminds me of an e-mail I sent out to a few thousand advisors back in 2006. After several years of growing interest in the resource sector (gold, mining, and metals stocks, and energy too), I began to see the signs of congestion building. Here's what I wrote:

> I've been getting many calls, asking my opinion about the hot resource market. This surprises me since my opinion is hardly worth the breath it takes

to express it. Opinions are like belly buttons: we all have them, but they're pretty much useless. (I concede that although they are useless, some can be quite sexy—both opinions and belly buttons.)

For what it's worth, my "opinion" was printed recently in the press in the May 11th issue of *Business Edge News Magazine*, "Portfolio manager sees correction in resource sector."

Things that worry me:

- Non-stop coverage of commodities on TV (in 2003, ROBTv [now BNN] refused to let me come on to talk about resources—who'd be interested?).
- Several equity issues per day from small mining companies.
- Strategy recommendations like, "This month we are raising our weightings half a percentage point in materials in light of recent gains in both gold and base metal prices."

This is the first time in a very long time that my picks don't include a mining company. If I'm right, I'll get a chance later on to reload commodity plays at better valuations, and if I'm wrong, it wouldn't be the first time.

You can probably determine from the above that I was getting out of the traffic. Like the border crossing experience, I suffered some flack from clients and others who had only just recently bought resource stocks (and probably too much of them). It felt like they too had their hands on their holsters and considered my comments akin to misbehaving in a "secure area." I did, however, manage to ride out the subsequent sell-off in all resource related stocks in comfort and later "get back on the road" by buying into the sector in early 2009 just prior to another run-up in the same stocks.

I finally reached my downtown Chicago hotel, where Al Capone gained notoriety in the 1920s. I think of his type of bad guy as "honest" crooks. It's not that I approve of their criminal activity. What I mean is that they were crooks and weren't really pretending to be otherwise. On the other hand, there have been many dishonest crooks in the corporate and investment world—crooks deliberately pretending to be honest businessmen. Get the difference? I think in many respects, crooks pretending to be good guys are worse than the Capone types. We will no doubt be discussing the odd criminal later in the book, but I digress.

While sitting in my Chicago hotel, it dawned on me that my border experience was a great example of the maverick way. Sure, I could have sat and toasted in line, but it just didn't make any sense. Despite having to go through more extensive border screening, I managed to avoid traffic. Was the delay worth it? I was comfortable, entertained, and after just a few minutes after getting back on the highway, I passed the motorhome that was at the very front of the line of vehicles I had escaped from. Another definition of *maverick*, found in Princeton University's WordNet, is: "Someone who exhibits independence in thought and action." There are situations when acting independent may be inappropriate, but it usually gets you where you need to go.

Where Does Traffic Come From?

At the border, traffic is caused by large numbers of vehicles trying to accomplish the same thing at once. It's a bottleneck by design. As long as everyone agrees to suffer the wait and humiliation, the country's government gets what it wants. The entire process is to create, control, and direct traffic to screen out undesirables to the exclusive benefit of a country's government. In a similar vein, financial businesses do their best to create, control, and direct traffic for their own financial benefit.

In most vehicular situations, traffic occurs rhythmically, such as during rush hours, but where and when market cycles occur—or the ebbs of flows of investment traffic—is almost impossible to predict. Furthermore, there is a significant difference between *predicting* and *anticipating*, as we'll explore later.

The beginnings of a flow of new traffic in the

investment game are quite random. Once traffic begins, however, there is no shortage of "experts" who claim to have predicted the change in flow and publish research and get media coverage to explain why it's happening after the fact.

Industry sectors all have unique rhythms correlated with one another and the overall economy, whether it's resources such as oil and gas, the communications industry, the technology sector, or dozens of others. Over time, as industries evolve, the nature of these extremely complex correlations can and often do change dramatically. Since we've already talked about how the buildup of traffic in the energy industry in the late '90s humbled my investment club, let's examine the stages of a more recent traffic jam in the same sector.

How Can You Tell If Investment Traffic Is Beginning?

While the so-called economic boom of the '90s was underway, there was relative stability in the price of oil following a brief spike in 1990 when Iraq invaded Kuwait. For most of the decade, prices averaged $18 to $20. No doubt the stability in the price of energy, such an important cost for every business and consumer, contributed to the booming economy. There wasn't much investor traffic again in the energy industry, as I recollect, until 2003, when oil prices began rising again. By 2005, the oil price had climbed well above the $50 mark.

A disruption in the supply of crude or a strong economy causing more demand for oil will mean rising prices of crude. (Crude is processed into gasoline and other petroleum-based commodities such as plastics.) Rising prices will bolster the fortunes of companies producing it.

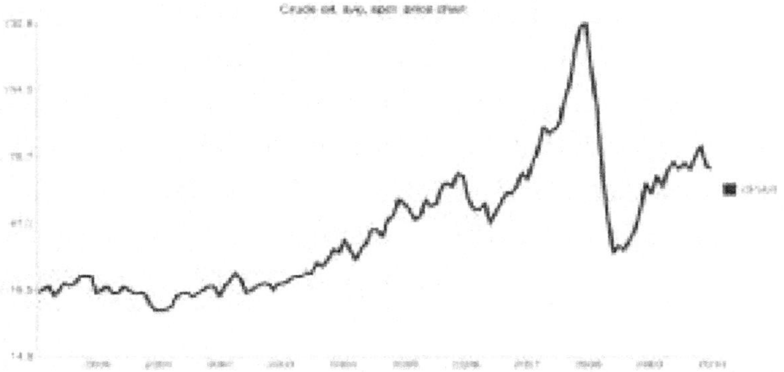

The interest in the oil sector germinates when those mavericks who bought the stocks when they were out of favour and cheap start making money. It gets the attention of other investors. It's not that the early buyers predicted that oil prices would skyrocket; it just made sense to buy the stocks cheap, and many were growing their revenues and earnings the hard way: discovering more oil wells and putting them into production. How does one know they're cheap? No matter how bad or boring things became for the industry, the stock prices just didn't go down anymore. Anyone who was a seller had finally sold.

The patient investor then buys in and just waits for something good to happen to attract traffic, and when it became evident that the price of oil had unexpectedly doubled, that seemed to do the trick.

Industry analysts gradually began to attribute the increase in price to all sorts of factors. The United States Department of Energy began publishing reports about the decline in petroleum reserves globally. Industry experts began talking about "peak oil," claiming that production had already reached its peak and would henceforth be shrinking indefinitely. Middle East tensions, Hurricane Katrina, and a host of other international events fuelled speculation that the price of oil would rocket to $200 or more per barrel.

Why does such a frenzy happen? Unadulterated greed is always the culprit. Investors want to get in on the action, and research analysts and industry gurus are suddenly popular and earning fees. The bigger the frenzy, the bigger the money movement. Research generates investor trading, which earns the investment firm commissions. Oil and gas companies and service companies tied to the industry's good fortune want to cash in by going public (initial public offerings, or IPOs) or raising funds doing debt and equity issues. This earns the financial community more juicy fees. People are suddenly keenly interested in investing in energy, which inspires the press to publish more and more information. A larger readership means more advertising revenues. Commodity funds (which invest in actual oil futures) offer retail and institutional investors even more ways to invest directly in oil, attract more assets under management, and earn more fees. Get the picture?

All this enthusiasm managed to drive the price of crude oil higher until it topped out at US$145. Early investors and even not-so-early buyers of energy stocks enjoyed quite a windfall. That is if they had the smarts to sell before the peak, because by 2008, it became clear that all of that hype was just that: hype. Worries about Iranian nuclear plants or North Korean missile tests weren't quite as important as the herd thought.

How Can You Tell When Investment Traffic Is About to Get Jammed?

Headlines.

When the published research and the press become outrageous, most investors are cramming to get onto the highway. Mavericks will be selling at a profit (perhaps a bit too early, but better safe than broke), and the Johnny-come-lately investors will be devastated.

If the message here is unclear, let me be blunt. It's okay to buy energy stocks while the price of oil is low, and even early on while it's trending higher. But you have to be ready to sell the stocks after they've gone up some, and just ignore the advice of friends, brokers, analysts, and the press. Be content that you made some money. When greed becomes your motivator, it's time to run for the hills. When you begin to believe you're a genius, and that every stock you touch turns to gold, *stop!* The complex array of circumstances that made the traffic go your way is impossible for even experts to fully understand. When your ego wants you to believe you've figured it all out, your ego is lying to you. Nothing goes up forever, and you must sell before things begin to go down. Bank your profits.

After all, economic theory and common sense dictate that if the price of oil rises so much that other industries dependent on oil can't make profits, and consumers must cut back their buying because they've spent all their discretionary cash on fuel, then economic growth must falter. Demand for oil then reverses and ultimately so does the price. The onset of global recession obliterates all the gains made in energy sector stocks much faster than they were earned.

On the other hand, if you didn't sell before the collapse in the oil price and energy stock prices, then you become a "*stuck*holder." My advice (to myself and others) is to take some time to reflect rather than sell in a panic. Oftentimes, the really good companies' stock prices plummet with the rest, and after things settle down, you might want to actually buy more shares in those companies. Sell the ones that were most obviously sucker stocks (i.e. you bought them without thinking, motivated mostly by greed) and use whatever money you can get for them to top up the good quality stocks.

Then be patient, perhaps for months or years. Never have all your money in one sector. You should invest other funds in other industries before they attract traffic. More about how to do this later in the guidebook.

The next chapter will examine other similar frenzies, often called "bubbles." I don't particularly like the term *bubble*, since it doesn't capture the dynamics of how they arise. The process really is more like a traffic jam, don't you think?

CHAPTER 3

AVOIDING INVESTMENT TRAFFIC JAMS, OR WHAT IS A "BUBBLE" ANYWAY?

Now that you're getting familiar with how a maverick investor thinks, it's important to understand that you're becoming part of a cult. Like a Harley enthusiast, you aren't popular with everyone, but you are part of a special group of people. Nothing illustrates this more than my last night in Chicago. I decided to go to a famous bar and steakhouse called Harry Caray's, where patrons can watch the Chicago Cubs play baseball on television no matter where they're standing or sitting.

I was wearing my customary uniform—a Harley T-shirt and jeans—and the bartender immediately came over and said, "Hi there, Harley guy!" I learned that her husband had three Harleys and that her parents had just returned from a trip along famed Route 66. They rode a Harley trike—a three-wheeler seemed sensible since the couple were in their seventies. (By the way, as you would expect in Chicago, the steak was delicious.)

The camaraderie of bikers, all of whom share the maverick code, is impossible to describe. Bikers wave at one another while driving by, approach one another for a chat while parked, and will without hesitation help one another out without being asked.

After dinner, I visited a nightclub with a great handle: Howl at the Moon. Duelling rock and roll pianos is the entertainment theme, but very talented young musicians also have drums and guitars at their disposal and can play any instrument. The starring duo were playing a ho-hum version of "Sweet Home Alabama" on two pianos, so I offered a generous tip if they'd allow me to accompany them on the drums to spice things up a bit. It was a hit, and I later played guitar and sang (okay, I use the term loosely) "Born to be Wild" and added some Canadian culture by performing Neil Young's "Rockin' in the Free World."

Several patrons thanked me for the show (they were no doubt drinking heavily), and a young fellow from New Hampshire came over to chat. That state is just riddled with mavericks. "Live Free or Die" is the state motto, and motorcycle helmets are not mandated. I was looking forward to riding in several of the western states where helmets are also optional.

Despite a bit of a hangover in the morning, the ride through the rest of Illinois and then Iowa to my next stop, Omaha, Nebraska, was a treat. I stopped for breakfast in Dixon, Illinois, which is the hometown of Ronald Reagan, a true maverick. Then I refuelled at the small town of De Soto, Iowa. I was certainly on a roll, since John Wayne, perhaps the king of mavericks, was born in the hamlet of Winterset, a stone's throw from the town.

In this part of the United States, the rolling hills sport miles of plush farmland and cattle, and the folks are friendly. Oh yes, and every once in a while, there's a thunderstorm—they're usually brief but very windy and wild.

My late dinner in Omaha was Nebraska corn chowder, corn on the cob, and a Nebraska pork chop. It's hard to sleep after a late heavy meal, but what helped ruin my rest was a lightning and thunder show outside my hotel window all night. It was like a fireworks display.

Traffic Jams of Note and the Warning Signs

"Fireworks" is an apt description of what happens when an industry group or investment theme gets to the point of ridiculous. Signs of investment fireworks include:

- It seems like nothing else is newsworthy in the financial press.
- Stock tips are coming from relatives or complete strangers.
- Friends will happily boast that they have invested all their money in one sector.
- People are outraged if you even hint at disagreeing about a sector outlook.

There have been several technology "bubbles" over the decades. In my early days, there was a period when IBM was considered invincible. Employees bragged about it being the only company that would hire you for life. Upstarts in computer and software related businesses went public in the early and later stages of these periods, and investors scrambled to buy them, bidding up stock prices. Microsoft Corporation was born in 1975. Another upstart, Apple Computer, Inc. (it dropped the word *Computer* from its name in 2007) was born in 1976. Compaq Computer Corporation emerged in 1982. I could go on, but you'd fall asleep in no time.

The most recent traffic jam in the sector occurred ten years ago now, although for old timers like me, it seems like yesterday. Many of these stocks trade on the NASDAQ exchange, and you can readily see how much money flowed onto the technology highway in the chart below. Note the arrow indicating where the index peaked on March 10, 2000, during the mother of all tech bubbles thus far.

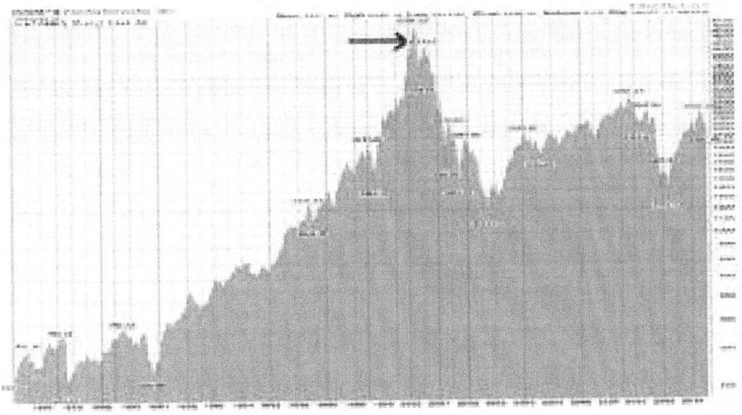

I'm not suggesting that maverick investors will avoid hot sectors. We made lots of money during those heydays in dozens of stocks. Once again, it's all about timing.

It was a crazy time, to be sure. Investors were frantically trying to buy IPOs, which seemed to rise on thin air. New methods of doing IPOs were tested. I recall a Linux networking company about to go public whose management team for some reason decided to do their first presentations in Toronto, Canada. Maybe they wanted to practice their presentation on bumpkins before going to the big cities such as New York. Many Broadway plays open in Toronto too before going to the big leagues.

The company's capital markets advisor had talked them into trying a Dutch auction approach. Normally the company's underwriter (an investment dealer) sets a price and shares are allocated on a first-come, first-served basis—sort of. In as simple terms as I can describe it, the Dutch auction goes like this: Interested buyers indicate how much they want to buy and at what price. Those who bid the highest price earliest get the most shares but only pay the lowest price that was offered by one of the bidders. Yes, it gives me a headache too.

I told them I'd buy the whole issue at a very generous price. Linux is an open-source operating system for computer geeks that was quickly becoming popular. In contrast, Microsoft and Apple use proprietary (private) operating systems to develop application software. Andover.Net was the company going public. It had created a networking portal that geeks can use to readily share programs they've developed.

It wasn't a really huge stock issue, and the firm I worked for managed lots of money, so I went big. I got a generous "fill," which means way more shares were allocated to my funds than a portfolio manager in faraway Canada should have expected. The stock price I paid on December 8, 1999, was US$18, and it rocketed up 252% that same day to close above US$63. The funds I managed all became the top performing mutual funds in Canada that year primarily because of this one windfall.

At the time, everybody and anybody was trying desperately to get in on this action every day and all day. I got lucky once, and a few others did too. The problem is individuals were throwing all their money at their brokers, looking for the big score, and that's just nuts. Professional money managers and capable investment advisors might dabble when an opportunity presents itself, but the lion's share of their investments would be well diversified into other areas.

One afternoon early in the year 2000, an associate and I decided to have lunch at a popular oyster bar. During the meal, the oyster shuckers kept disappearing into the kitchen where there was a telephone, where they could call their broker to buy and sell technology stocks. They were even suggesting stock tips to patrons without realizing that some of us were professional money managers. A great sign of a bubble is when taxi drivers, your relatives, and even oyster shuckers have got on the bandwagon and are investing in the same type of stocks. If everyone owns it and everyone decides to sell, who's going to be left to buy it?

Oyster shuckers trading tech stocks *during* work hours was proof enough to me that the fireworks had begun, and when every last firecracker was spent, it would be the end of a glorious bubble. It was time to steer clear of the heavy traffic. When we returned to the office, we began selling every tech stock we held in portfolios. It wasn't long afterward that it was all over but the crying. The all-time technology peak for the tech sector occurred on March 10, 2000, and the next day the stock prices began tumbling. And then 9/11 hit and put a pin in the rest of the market's balloon the following year, resulting in a deep recession.

The signs of when a bubble or bull market is in its late stages should be clearer to you now. When exactly will it end? It's impossible to tell. In a speech in 1996, Alan Greenspan, the Chairman of the Federal Reserve in the U.S. at the time, coined the now-famous phrase "irrational exuberance." He used the expression to describe the questionable optimism shared by investors at the time. Greenspan was a maverick, and although his anxiety proved to be just a few years too early, he successfully identified the beginning signs of a massive traffic jam in the making. He foretold the coming bust in the technology bubble and subsequent recession.

I recall listening to Greenspan present at a luncheon meeting several years later, and his topic was the developing housing bubble in the U.S. market. He was again anticipating a gathering traffic jam. This time it ultimately ended in the U.S. housing and mortgage meltdown that caused the more recent financial crisis and recession.

Avoiding heavy traffic or going against the flow before the traffic jam ends in a pileup is an important rule when it comes to maverick investing. If you can identify trouble signs in advance, you'll never end up having to panic. And you must never panic, right? So how does a maverick investor blaze a trail that won't be congested and laden with misleading signs or directions? The key is to go your own way based on smart thinking rather than avarice.

Trailblazer: a pioneer, or somebody
who makes a new path through a wilderness.

PART TWO

WHAT A MAVERICK INVESTOR KNOWS

CHAPTER 4

TRAILBLAZING, OR GO YOUR OWN WAY!

The morning ride towards Denver, Colorado, began with a thundershower, but it cleared quickly and the sun was soon shining. Riding through prairies is not very interesting when it comes to scenery, but it's a whole lot of fun on a bike made for cruising. It was a pleasure to drive on highways with a posted speed limit of 75 mph (roughly 120 km/h). As you'd expect in America's heartland, the speed limit is pretty much the same as the speed you'd be driving ordinarily. I think it's a reflection of the fact that people in this part of the country are honest. Why is it so common to have speed limits of 55 mph (88 km/h) or 100 km/h (62 mph) when nobody drives at that snail's pace?

Since the roads are straight and with few vehicles, my speed varied from 87 mph (or 140 km/h, which was an easier number to lock onto with my metric speedometer) when it wasn't raining. I sped up to 99 mph (or 160 km/h) when it was raining. I figured no state trooper in his right mind would want to get wet just to issue a speeding ticket.

Distractions were most welcome. I drove by a camel of all things, and thought to myself, "I'd like to meet the maverick who brought this creature to Nebraska."

To break up the journey, I stopped to visit an original Pony Express station in Gothenburg, Nebraska (the town founded in 1882 by Olof Bergstrom, who named the town after a city in Sweden).

Once I entered Colorado, the terrain changed significantly. Subtly rolling hills with grass that was no longer bright green, but rather light brown, were populated by huge herds of cattle and sometimes herds of horses just as large. Passing by massive cattle ranches commingled with irrigated fields growing a variety of crops makes you feel like this is indeed the gateway to God's country. Just before I reached Denver, lightning displays forewarned that thundershowers were imminent, so I put on some rain gear. I continued on and was soon transported from ranchland to metropolis in what seemed like the blink of an eye.

Before retiring after my long ride, I consumed a delightfully generous portion of the best prime rib I've ever tasted.

What else do you eat in cattle country? After dinner, I was in the bar, and a woman sitting nearby came over to invite me to the table she and her business associate were sitting at.

"I saw you and knew you rode a bike. My friend suggested that just because you have a Harley T-shirt doesn't mean you ride, but I told her that anyone who rides can spot someone else who rides easily and the T-shirt has nothing to do with it," she explained.

The lady's name was Deborah, and she said that her man had passed away recently of cardiac arrest. He was only in his forties. Although she had her motorcycle license and could drive herself, she always preferred touring on the back of his bike. She had been trying to explain to her friend what it's like to ride and how she missed it, but when she saw me, she thought I could contribute to the conversation. I tried, but there's a saying that bikers have: "If I have to explain, you wouldn't understand." The truth is, a maverick loves the company of likeminded others but isn't really interested in recruiting. Kind of the opposite of a Jehovah's Witness.

Her associate would never understand unless she experienced the ride herself. I certainly sympathized with Deborah's pain. She not only lost her husband, she was separated from her other passion too. I felt like asking her to get on the back of my Harley and ride with me to the coast, but she probably wasn't quite ready for that yet. She gave me her contact info, so maybe when I'm in Houston (her hometown) or if she's ever in Canada, I can give her the gift of freedom again.

How Does a Maverick Identify a Trail Worth Blazing?

Before trailblazing through the investment wilderness, it's important to have a firm understanding what *risk* really means. It's not nearly as simple as industry pundits would have the public believe.

Taking a Harley onto an ATV trail is not just risky, it's crazy. Riding a dirt bike on the same trail isn't nearly as risky, unless you don't know how to handle one. Walking the same trail is the least risky alternative, but it will take forever to get anywhere. And that's assuming you haven't a heart condition, which would make taking the trail under any circumstances risky.

Most people are risk averse, whether they admit it or not. My mushroom farmer from the Introduction thought he could deal with volatility and discovered he could only stomach very favourable (upward) volatility, not the bad kind. For some reason, even so-called experts consider volatility risky. Surely my mushroom farmer would agree that upward volatility is in many ways the opposite of risk?

I don't have to tell you there's risk associated with everything we do, from leaving the front door of your home to skydiving. A skydiver, who is fanatic about safety while engaging in the sport, will probably be subject to much less risk than the average person leaving their home in a given day.

Myth: Short-term investments secured by assets are the least risky.

In case you were hibernating, the recent financial crisis was caused by banks, insurance companies, and investment dealers packaging and pawning off short-term securities backed by mortgages and a host of derivatives. Asset-backed commercial paper (ABCP) was supposed to be low risk, and most investors who bought these securities were frequently told and believed they were risk-free. When the assets behind the securities are risky, and all assets have some risk associated with them, then so is the short-term paper to some extent.

Depositing money in the bank or in money market funds and the like will generally be much less *volatile*. But just like walking the ATV trail will take forever to get anywhere, it is going to take forever to make a significant rate of return on your money, if you make a return at all. A maverick investor considers a low return on investment risky. The risk of a low return may be worth it if there are short-term plans for the funds, including buying a new car or a house, or going on vacation. Subjecting your money to more volatility would mean not having all the money available at a closing date or at vacation time.

Myth: The stock market is risky.

I hope you're now convinced that the stock market isn't risky in and of itself. It's risky at those times when everyone believes it's safe. When you read a headline like this one I saw on Monday, July 20, 2010, in *USA Today*, "Earnings hopes help market gain a bit," then the broader stock market is probably not at a risky stage at all. In fact, I also read in the same paper on the same day: "U.S. housing starts tumbled a larger-than-expected 5.0% to 549,000 in June, reinforcing a theme played out by virtually every other housing market number of late."

I will translate these mixed messages into "maverick-speak" for you. Reporters have no idea what's going on, but despite what should be very bad news in the housing market, the stock market's reaction wasn't negative. So why not just make up a *story* to justify the climb in the market such as "investors are hoping" that earnings of companies that haven't even reported yet will be better than expected, which might explain the strong performance from stocks. *Yikes!*

You can read the papers and listen to the business news yourself and come to your own judgement about the general investment mood. In the example above, it was still trendy to be pessimistic, and it shows in how the media presents events. If the stock market, which generally "leads" the economy, is flat or rising even amongst really bad news, such as weak employment statistics, sluggish GDP growth, and lousy earnings reports, then it is not a risky time to be invested. If your advisor or friends tell you it's risky "because" of this news? Put on your maverick hat and pretend to agree with them, but if you believe as I do that upward volatility is the opposite of risk, then why not get some of it?

As I get older, I have trouble recalling the dozens of instances where risk was at a minimum for the domestic stock market, overseas markets, bond markets, particular industries, or individual stocks. The following example I do remember vividly. Sometime in 1998, I was sitting in the boardroom with my associates at a firm foolish enough to hire me. The Asian Financial Crisis had just devastated stock markets in the Far East. It's not important to understand what caused the crisis, and nobody does fully understand anyway, but you can find all sorts of retrospective theories from armchair experts if you care to do some research on the Internet.

Our senior managers at the firm had invested some of our institutional clients' money in a fund specializing in Asian markets a few months before the bottom fell out. Yes, even professional fund managers come late to a party. Like most senior managers, they had no interest in the opinion of us junior portfolio managers, so they hadn't consulted with us about the initiative. Asian markets had been performing extremely well for a few years, and when our boys discovered they weren't "in the flow," they just had to try and squeeze into heavy traffic. When the traffic jammed up in July 1997, a whole bunch of client money was lost.

When we were in that boardroom meeting, the worst of the crisis was already far behind us. My maverick instincts told me that it might be a good time to invest in Asia again, and in this meeting, I became convinced the risk pendulum had swung the other way and Asian markets were no longer risky. The clincher was when a senior manager stated, "We're never going to invest in Asia ever again; I can promise you that!" Messages like these are music to the ears of mavericks. If the consensus is so thoroughly against going in a direction, there's a trail to blaze.

From that point forward, the most generous returns have come from Asian markets, and China in particular has been the undisputed leader in global growth.

Truth: Actual minimum risk occurs when perceived risk is at a maximum.

My previous book, *Resources Rock*, was inspired by an investment advisor client. I had determined as early as 2002 that developing economies were going to absorb resources such as copper, coal, iron ore, nickel, zinc, and other commodities like a gigantic sponge absorbs water. So I promptly launched a mutual fund dedicated to resources. When I presented the fund to the advisor as something that would make money for his clients, he said, "I lost my shirt in gold and other junior mining stocks once already, and I'll never buy them again." Perhaps my book didn't sell like hotcakes, but the resource fund would have made his clients quite happy. The mutual fund was launched in June 24, 2002, just as the world was about to come out of a deep global recession, fuelled by growing economies in the Far East. Demand for resources and the prices of resource stocks rocketed higher for several years from that point forward.

Riding along roads infrequently travelled can be rewarding. My leaving the congestion of Denver and reaching higher altitudes was refreshing. The mountain scenery was nothing short of spectacular, and I enjoyed a respite from the summer heat. It's much cooler at 7,800 feet above sea level. A detour from the Interstate was thrilling, with roads twisting and turning through mountain passes, and it allowed me to even out the wear and tear on my tires—the long flat prairie roads wore out the bottom, while the mountains put at least some wear on the sidewalls.

Descending into Utah returned me to the blazing dry desert heat characteristic of most of the state. It is sparsely populated, so you do really feel like a maverick on its highways. Despite being less comfortable, the benefits of travelling on secluded roadways are many. You decide how fast or slow you'd like to drive, rather than being pushed or cajoled by traffic one way or another.

Going your own way, however, also has its unique inconveniences that a maverick must tolerate. I didn't really need fuel yet, but I randomly decided to rest and top up the tank at one of the few service stations in the middle of nowhere. I got back on the road, and about three miles out, there was a sign that said there'd be no more services for the next 100 miles.

If I hadn't just happened to gas up, I would either have had to turn around and go back for fuel in 110 degree weather or run out of gas in no man's land. Either scenario might have made me a bit grumpy. You'd think someone would realize that the sign belongs *before* the service station instead of after, where it would be useful information *and* convenient. After more than 400 miles (about 640 km), I stopped for the night in the tiny hamlet of Marysvale, Utah.

If you use an advisor or have an online trading account and get access to published research, you will notice that they publish "signs" that are often misplaced as well. Do you ever wonder how a research analyst suddenly puts out a sell recommendation after the stock has already plummeted?

Going your own way when it comes to your investments will also have stumbling blocks. Waiting for your investment decisions to work can be like riding a long stretch of highway with no service centres in sight for miles. Other investors will be boasting how much they're making every day playing in heavy traffic while you're barely coasting along on your own trail. It's funny how those same people never talk about what they've lost getting stuck in traffic jams time and again. They tend to only discuss their most recent and probably infrequent wins.

Occasionally there will be roadblocks and unexpected detours, but the maverick knows to stay calm and rational and will deal with these problems when they arise.

Be Careful When Asking for Directions

The investment industry is a business. As mentioned earlier, it is in the best financial interest of many advisors—and certainly their employers such as banks, insurance companies, and fund marketing companies—to control you. You are revenue. Depending upon the primary source of income for these businesses, they will want you to invest the way that best maximizes their own revenue.

For pure investment dealers or stockbrokers, who make most of their money from trading commissions, IPO fees, and selling bonds or secondary issues (stock issued by companies that are already public for the purpose of raising funds), it's best *for them* if you do buy into market bubbles: increasing trading activity in stocks and bonds that are over-valued. Even if you sell in a panic when the market is dropping, they benefit. These businesses earn commissions in either case.

This conflict of interest is supposedly why we have security regulators. In recent years, the regulators have gone overboard to the point where the burden of regulation discourages all of us from making money. And now that larger financial services conglomerates own their own investment dealers, they discourage their former stockbrokers (now called "advisors") from excessive trading activity or risk anyway because even the subsidiary company must contribute to the master plan of the parent.

The larger banks and insurance companies, most now owning their own investment dealer subsidiaries, would like nothing better than to have your investments less volatile and secure even if they don't grow at all. If your money just stays put, they can consistently charge you fees, forecast their revenues based on those fees, and invest revenues in real estate and other assets that will make more money for the firm.

I am not being critical of these companies, just realistic. All the services they provide (consumer and corporate banking, mortgage lending, international funds transfers, and so forth) wouldn't be available if they weren't in business, and to be in business requires them to behave as businesses.

Of course, they don't mind if your investments grow a little. It is a nice bonus for financial services companies if your money grows just enough to pay their fees. However it is not *necessary* for your money to grow, and if it shrinks (reducing their revenues and profits), all they need to do is spend money (which they earned from charging you fees) on advertising sexy new services and investment funds, encouraging more customers to sign up.

There is no shortage of advice telling you which trail you should follow. The way the advice, or "directions," are presented can be very persuasive. Millions of dollars are spent on talented marketing professionals to make them persuasive.

On my way to Nevada in the morning, I travelled about 100 miles and decided it was time for breakfast. Signs for McDonald's, Denny's, and other chains riddled the highway, and admittedly, it's tempting even for the maverick type to just pick one.

It was at least 100°F (roughly 38°C) as I descended into the desert, and any place with air conditioning sounded glorious. I resisted the temptation to just follow the advice on the billboards and took the exit for Cedar City, Utah, hoping to find the *right* sort of restaurant for me. It wasn't long before I spotted the Main Street Grill. The food was delicious, young pretty ladies waited on me at my table, and I left feeling I'd been somewhere special. No billboards for this restaurant were on the freeway; I had to look and find the place.

The best investment opportunities are just like that. You have to look in order to find them. If someone is beating down your door to offer you the best investment ever, nine times out of ten it will prove to be very disappointing. If it's such a great idea, why are they telling you? Whenever this happens to me, my maverick senses begin to tingle. When

I'm being sold to, my blood runs cold.

Things to help guide you when trailblazing with your savings:

- It's your money, and you can invest it how you want.
- Don't let others influence your better judgement.
- Risk is a good thing at the right times.
- Look for opportunities; they aren't going to walk through the door.

It's roughly 400 miles (643 kilometres) from Marysvale, Utah, to Las Vegas, but it certainly seemed much longer. As I descended (in altitude) from Cedar City, it became hotter and I felt I was in hell on earth. I passed briefly through a corner of Arizona, and the thermometer on my bike read 120°F (49°C), which may not be 100% accurate, but this temperature is just not what a Canadian is used to. There wasn't a cloud in the sky, and although in these states, I *can* ride with no helmet, I put mine back on just so I'd have a bit of shade.

When I crossed into Nevada, I saw the first casino within seconds. I parked the bike and ran inside to try to get my body temperature down. I sat down for a half hour and I was still perspiring.

Heading back to my wheels to saddle up, some folks came over to chat when they saw the license plates on my Harley. From Calgary, the couple explained they had endeavored to rent a Harley (he owned a Yamaha or something Japanese back home) and they had hoped to ride to the Valley of Fire, Lake Mead, and the Hoover Dam. I've been doing that ride myself for years and I never get tired of it, but then I do it in the winter time. They lasted about twenty minutes in traffic in the scorching heat and then returned the bike without even leaving the city of Las Vegas.

What would a maverick do? I decided on the spot that I'd avoid the city traffic of Las Vegas altogether and rode straight through to the little town of Pahrump, Nevada. As we'll discuss in the next chapter, it's imperative that when riding or investing you be prepared to adjust your route quickly when circumstances dictate.

CHAPTER 5

GAMBLING OR INVESTING?

A casino is a bit like the financial industry. The objective is to convince you that you are going to be a winner, to help get you in the door. It doesn't matter if you play slot machines, craps, or blackjack, the casino has programmed every game to work the same way:

- You occasionally win something, which is thrilling for anybody.
- The thrill is pleasing, which keeps you betting.
- Over time, you lose more than you win.
- Your money is now their money.

There's a good reason why a genius capable of counting cards is shunned. Card counters are not playing the game upon which the casino thrives.

My brother-in-law and I were having a powwow over cocktails in the fall of 2008, just when the automakers were begging governments for funding to help them stay afloat. He explained that since Ford seemed to be in the best shape financially that it would be wise to buy it cheap. (I was so proud of him.) The stock had broken below the $2 level at the time.

I had soon forgotten all about it, but recently asked how it worked out. He told me his broker, who works for the investment dealer subsidiary of a large bank, was "not allowed" to let him buy it. It seems that the stock was fine to buy before the automakers ran into difficulties, trading between \$5 and \$10 for years. When it fell to all-time lows, however, it was deemed too *risky* by the firm and its compliance people (who have never managed a penny or published a research report) at a paltry \$2 or less.

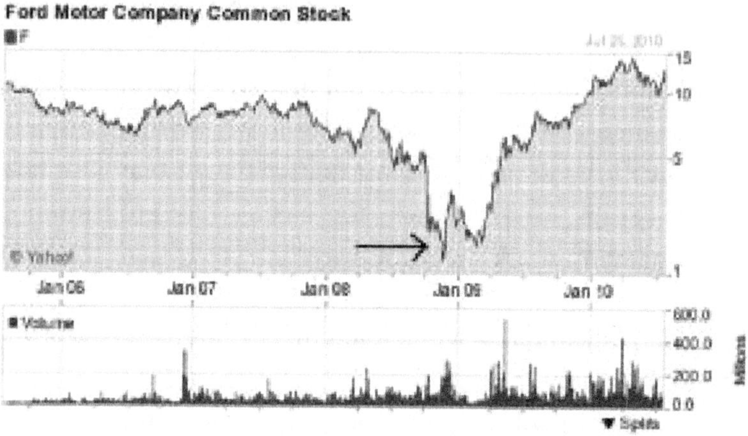

He did end up buying the stock at a later date for \$4.66. It seems compliance people are okay with you missing much of the upside, as long as they don't have their own necks on the line. While the stock is dropping, it is deemed "too risky" for their employers' reputations, but not when it's been going up already. The stock since then rose to above \$10 by December of 2009 and got above \$13 in 2010.

Both novice and self-proclaimed "experienced" investors avidly read what the experts are doing and often copy them. The excerpt below as posted on December 30, 2008, by Michelle Krebs on the Edmunds Auto Observer website, which was around the same time my brother-in-law first shared his investment idea with me:

> On Tuesday—just in time to take year-end losses—Kerkorian sold the last of his investment in Ford. The move came just six months after Kerkorian's Tracinda Corp. bought a 6.49 stake in Ford and carries with it deep losses.

It is not a good idea to take for granted that a rich person garnering lots of publicity makes brilliant decisions every day. It's possible they've allowed their ego to get the better of them, which is fine, I suppose, if you are wealthy and can afford to make mistakes as big as your ego.

In my estimation, my brother-in-law was *investing*. Kerkorian the investment guru was more likely *gambling*, and when his ill-timed bet went sour, he bailed. My brother-in-law still owns his Ford stock at the time of writing this book. I can assure you that Kerkorian did much more research than did my brother-in-law. Later in the guidebook, I will explain why more information does not make for better decisions.

Perhaps Kerkorian identified his error and wanted to quickly get back to his maverick roots. It's okay to admit you are wrong and regroup. The sale of his stake in Ford, which lost hundreds of millions of dollars, may have been a calculated repositioning, as the investment climate had surely changed. I can't read minds, but just as I had to get out of Nevada to find a cooler climate, perhaps the investment guru had to abandon one idea in order to have the cash to exploit another "better" investment idea. I will also address this sort of reaction to mistakes or dramatic shifts in trends later in the book.

Oh, and this is an excerpt from the blog Zero Hedge, posted on March 2, 2009, which I found entertaining:

> For anyone still caring to listen to Cramer's recommendations, we present the case of Foster Wheeler, which Cramer said was a "buy, buy, buy" at $80, and mentioned it about twenty times over the past year on its ceaseless way down as one of his all time top picks. Please indulge in the company's one-year stock chart. As Cramer said early last year, "Many of you say 'the stock is at [$75 post split] it's over': Stay tuned—there's much more ahead".... Oh yeah, Jimbo, much more pain and destruction ahead.
>
> Indicatively, it closed today at $12.88.
>
> [Note: I did not bother to include the chart.]

What inspires people to act upon the advice of celebrities or personalities on television? Tooting horns and ringing bells are evidence of showmanship, not investment acumen. If you think it through, as a maverick should, then you should conclude that the most astute and learned professional investors are not likely to be sharing their hard-earned knowledge with the general public for no fee. But thanks to those who blog or complain about the so-called advice they foolishly act upon—whether they've heard it on the radio, seen it on TV, or read about it in a newsletter—anyone with a song and a dance can turn poorly researched random rants about investment topics into entertainment. The audience makes it a show.

There's a huge difference between investing and entertainment. I was regularly a guest on business television, and callers would ask my opinion about various stocks. I began by being brutally honest, which I determined didn't sit well with the caller. The callers were a bit thick at times, and I eventually realized that if they asked my opinion about a particular stock, they probably just bought it. My responses became more temperate as follows:

- *Early days' response if I didn't like the stock:* "I think stock is too expensive and company management incompetent. Don't own it." (There then would be an eerie silence from the caller afterwards.)
- *Later days' response if I didn't like the stock:* "I'd prefer to buy this one much cheaper, so if you already own it, I'd sell if it goes higher or wait for a correction before I'd buy some more."

Why hurt someone's feelings about a decision that's already made? I discovered my job on the show was entertaining viewers rather than giving advice. Not all viewers saw it that way. One caller was in a fury about an opinion I'd offered months before:

> I just called to say you should be fired from your job as a portfolio manager. Last time I called and asked about Research in Motion [makers of the now popular BlackBerry mobile device], you said, and I quote, "Back up the truck." The stock price is $30 and still going down.

When I said, "Back up the truck," the stock price was $60 in a buoyant market and RIM was about to release good sales numbers. I sold perhaps a month or two later at $80, because mavericks aren't greedy, even though it continued to climb to north of $100. My advice—or, rather, "commentary"—on the TV was a snapshot of what I was doing at a point in time. Clearly, the caller didn't understand this.

I wasn't particularly delicate, and replied on air, "I think it's foolish to make investment decisions based on what somebody says on TV!" I don't think I was ever invited back on the show.

As an aside, I was CEO of the company I founded, but despite this, I did on many occasions notionally fire myself as portfolio manager and assign the job of managing a particular fund to a seasoned veteran I had hired or a youngster I trained (and would supervise them more closely than the others until they got their legs). I handed off the resources mutual fund we've talked about already to a promising young portfolio manager, and kept an eye on his progress while occasionally pulling rank on decision-making. When the fund won the Lipper Award for its incredible performance in 2009, he was subsequently recruited by our competitors. It's always rewarding to teach a younger ranch hand some tricks and see him move on to a new ranch where he can be the top cowboy.

As it turned out, I was much closer to the California border than I thought. (I seldom look at maps since I can no longer read without glasses and rely on GPS in my old age.) Much of the morning ride was still in desert territory, but as I slowly got further into California, the temperature dropped at least 10°F or 15°F and a nice breeze soothed my sunburned epidermis.

I stopped for gas and was surprised to find I was only three miles away from an old ghost town that had been restored. The town of Calico was named for the variety of colours seen when looking at King Mountain. It was said the colours were "as purty as a gal's calico skirt." This is how the town got its name. Its peak population was 3,000, supported by the Maggie Mine, which between the years 1881 and 1907 produced up to an estimated $20 million in silver and $9 million in other materials, but the end came to the silver rush in 1896 and Calico not long after became a ghost town.

From that point on, the California landscape became increasingly more beautiful and the climate more comfortable. I decided to head towards my namesake, Malibu (pronounced *Mal*-i-bu). Like a portfolio, a Harley needs to be serviced regularly and so I popped into a nearby dealership for an oil change. The ride from the Ventura Freeway through the Santa Monica Mountains was breathtaking, especially when you suddenly see you're approaching the ocean in front of you. Once I checked into my hotel and discovered there was a surfing competition underway, I decided staying an extra day in Malibu wouldn't kill me.

How to Tell the Difference Between Investing and Gambling

I asked a very smart friend of mine to preview some chapters of this guidebook, and she provided some excellent tips but posed the difficult question: "How do you develop 'smart thinking' and when do you know you've got 'avarice'?"

My instinctive response would be: "You always know when you're being greedy. You just want someone else to say that your greed is okay." Well, I'll say it then: greed is okay. The proviso is that you fully understand when greed is motivating your decision and live with the consequences. Avarice is driven by desire, which is not a trait of a maverick investor.

Remember, it's best if investment decisions are rational and stripped of emotion. Greed is associated with elation on the one hand, and anger (usually directed at oneself) on the other hand.

When decisions are motivated by greed, I call it gambling. In my mind, there are different sorts of gamblers. Some gamblers place modest bets, and if they win, they move along to another game. For me this might be roulette. There are those who enjoy playing one game they're good at, such as blackjack or craps, hoping for a big score. Finally, there are those who are addicts. I can't help those folks, so let's assume we're just discussing the first two types.

It's okay to do a bit of gambling with a modest part of your disposable income. In fact, maverick investors can apply some of what they know and have fun too. Unlike the casinos, financial markets have no limits or games stacked in favour of the house. It's the Wild West, and if a maverick understands herd behaviour and the merits of contrarian thinking, and does some research, the results can be quite lucrative.

Whether using stocks, bonds, options, hedge funds, domestic mutual funds, foreign equity or debt funds, or commodity exchange-traded funds (if you don't know what these things are and want to know, buy a book), or whatever, maverick principles will help you be more successful. To put it plainly: counting cards may not be allowed in a casino, but anything goes when it comes to markets. Just don't forget the important lessons we covered earlier. Most of the financial industry is trying to make your money their money. There's a reason why a cowboy sleeps with his boots on and his gun within reach.

The fine line between gambling and investing is hard even for old cowhands to pinpoint. Investing also involves bets, but the bets are calculated. Every decision a maverick investor makes involves a calculated bet—whether it's to be in the market or not at all, biasing a portfolio in favour of stocks versus bonds, skewing stock selection in favour of one or several industry groups, or picking individual stocks or other types of securities.

I met a lady once in line at a convenience store. She bought a handful of lottery tickets, and I asked her, "Aren't the odds of winning pretty remote for those lotteries?"

Her reply was, "The odds are good. There's a fifty/fifty chance of me winning."

Confused, I asked, "How do you figure?"

I laughed aloud when she said, "Either I win or I lose; that's fifty/fifty, isn't it?"

A maverick investor knows there's always a probability that any decision to buy or sell or hold can prove to be incorrect. The objective is to minimize that probability as much as is feasible. It's impossible to make it zero.

This is why financial firms have sold so many "guaranteed" funds lately. People love the *idea*, however impossible, of being allowed to gamble with no chance of losing. Whenever there's a promise that you won't lose or some other similar guarantee, my maverick senses begin to tingle. There's usually a promise of significant upside potential and a guarantee that at worst you'll get all (or a portion) of your original investment back. Many investors a few years ago bought so-called guaranteed funds only to find that the best they ever did receive was the guaranteed amount (extremely disappointing) or much less after the fees were paid to the company offering the product. If you think this stuff is new, trust me, it's not.

A fancy formula-based strategy back in the '80s called "portfolio insurance" was popular for a brief period. An estimated $60 billion of institutional money was invested in this form of "dynamic hedging." It isn't important to know how the math works. Basically, if a particular asset class (stocks, bonds, or short-term securities) goes up, then you could "afford" to take more risk because you are richer on paper anyway, so the program would then buy more of a good thing. If this better-performing asset class suddenly stopped performing, you simply sold it quickly to lock in your profits. The problem was that all these programs wanted to sell stocks on the same day, and as we've discussed earlier in the book, when everyone decides they want to sell and there are no buyers, you get a stalemate.

The "insurance" might have worked if you actually *could* sell the securities just because you wanted to, but if you can't sell, you suffer along with everyone else—the notional guarantee isn't worth the paper it's printed on. Remember these are markets, and even though you see a price in the newspaper or on your computer screen for a stock, there's no trade unless someone will step up to buy stock from you. The market crash that began on Black Monday—October 19, 1987—was, in my opinion, fuelled by portfolio insurance programs. The market was going down, so the programs began selling stocks all at once. There weren't nearly enough buyers to trade with. By the end of October, stock markets in Hong Kong had fallen 45.5%, and others had fallen as follows: Australia 41.8%, Spain 31%, the U.K. 26.4%, the U.S. 22.7%, and Canada 22.5%.

Minimizing the Probability of Stupidity

If you're gambling, follow the same steps you would as if you were investing. If it's a particular stock you are anxious to own, do some homework, or at least look at someone else's research available through your broker or on the Internet. When I was young, there were limited means to learn about a company. I would have to call the company and ask for a hardcopy annual report to be sent to me. When it arrived after several days, I'd study it a bit so I didn't sound too ignorant, then I'd call and try to get an executive (controller, VP finance, or investor relations manager) to talk to me. If asking questions didn't satisfy my need to know, then I'd ask to come and meet with them in the flesh. Nowadays, you have all the information you need at your fingertips.

Getting the information is one thing, developing an opinion is something altogether different. If you read analyst reports for your preparation, ignore their opinions or recommendations. Your broker will hate you for it, but don't forget that he has a different objective than you do. Your broker (his analyst too) wants to keep his job and so the recommendation will have been polluted by many layers of middle management. You just want the info.

I remember doing it the hard way many years ago. After reading a company's terrible earnings report in the newspaper, I decided to learn more. I discovered the stock was ridiculously cheap, and perhaps deservedly so because they weren't making money. I called to talk to someone and got the CEO.

He said, "Why would anyone want to buy stock in this company?" At the time, interest rates were extraordinarily high (President Ronald Reagan had been fighting inflation by keeping rates high), which had hurt the housing market. The company was a manufacturer of "white goods," or large appliances such as refrigerators and ovens—of course they'd been struggling.

At that time, Reagan was winning the inflation battle and interest rates had already begun a slow decline from high double-digit levels. My reasoning was that once people began buying homes again, they'd buy appliances. Once inflation was defeated and interest rates began falling, there was a vibrant housing boom and not only was the company suddenly doing very well, it was bought by a larger company at a price that was a great deal higher than what it was when I first made that telephone call.

In this case, even the CEO was the wrong person to ask for an opinion. All I needed to know was why things were so bad, and this info he provided. Whether he believed things would get better didn't matter. His judgement was biased by his emotional state.

Actually, the opinions of CEOs can be suspect on many things. I recall meeting with the CEO of a newspaper conglomerate in the early '80s. I suggested they might want to consider getting into electronic media since personal computers were catching on. He said, "We don't believe there are enough PCs out there; it's just a fad." Within two weeks, his newspaper published a story about a study that found 30% of Canadian households already had a PC. It made me laugh.

Okay, just one more example. Sitting with the CEO of a cable television company, I remarked on how much capital Ted Rogers (CEO and founder of Rogers Communications) was devoting to wireless telephony when coverage was sparse and the cellular phones were heavier than a jug of milk. He claimed it was ridiculous to think that people would want a wireless phone when there are perfectly good wired telephones installed everywhere. Funny stuff!

Rely on your own judgement and not the opinions of others!

Be careful though: you might arrive at your decision using bad information. When working for a larger investment counselling firm, I used a similar line of reasoning, and after digging through as much publicly available information as I could find, I convinced my associates we should consider buying one of the banks in the northeast United States. It was the tail end of the savings and loan crisis, which you don't have to know much about, but savings and loans (S&Ls) were specialized banks that used low-interest, but federally insured, deposits in savings accounts to fund mortgages.

Things got tough for these banking businesses when higher interest rates became available from a variety of other sources, such as the growing popularity of money market mutual funds back then. The rates the S&Ls were allowed by regulators to pay on deposits weren't high enough to attract depositors.

The regulations were relaxed in 1982, which overnight allowed them to make loans, pay higher interest on deposits, and so on. Banks even began getting involved in activities they weren't very good at, such as speculating in real estate and commercial loans. Many of the banks began losing serious money, and by 1989, the President and Congress introduced bailout measures. (Does all this sound vaguely familiar?)

Between the years 1986 and 1995, over a thousand banks, totalling in assets of over $500 billion, failed. By 1999, the crisis cost $153 billion, with taxpayers footing the bill for $124 billion and the S&L industry paying the rest.

My thinking was that surviving banks might be a good investment because, by golly, the stocks were cheap. I researched the Bank of New England and Bank of Boston. To top it off, I went to visit the Bank of New England's management. My efforts to try to see Bank of Boston people were to no avail. They wouldn't see me.

Management of the bank convinced me things were just fine, and they showed me data to support the claim. We bought a good position in the stock, but, to my chagrin, the stock just kept going down. At this stage, my ego got the better of me. I should've admitted something was amiss, sold the stock, and moved on.

Within a few months, in 1991, the Bank of New England Corporation was seized by the Federal Deposit Insurance Corporation (FDIC) because of heavy losses in its loan portfolio and it was placed into Chapter 7 liquidation. At the time, it was the 33rd largest bank in the U.S., and its federal seizure bailout was the second largest on record. At its peak, it had been the 18th largest bank and had over 470 branch offices. *Ouch!*

If my memory serves me, the other one I'd considered, Bank of Boston, recovered and would have made a guru out of me instead of an idiot.

What went wrong? Management in no uncertain terms lied to my face. It isn't the first or last time over my thirty years it would happen either. Mavericks take for granted that other people are honest. It's better to be burned on rare occasions than to have to live life distrusting everyone. However, the episode did teach me to be more discerning when listening to potentially conflicted managers later in life. Despite the mistruths delivered to me, I still hold myself accountable. When things weren't going *my* way, I really should have gone *away*.

The S&L financial crisis took its toll on stock markets, just as our recent financial crisis did. Experience is a glorious thing. In the midst of the more recent crisis, on February 9, 2008, I sent this note out to advisor clients of mine:

> Just in case these numbers get scrambled on their way to you, three years after the S&L crisis occurred, the stock market had appreciated 83.3%. Of course, a whole new crisis (October '87) was to hit a few years later, but I believe the point is made.

Period	Simple Return	Annualized Return
1 year later	13.5%	13.5%
2 years later	50.1%	22.5%
3 years later	83.3%	22.4%

Have I mentioned markets *always* recover? I cannot emphasize it enough!

If your bets aren't working, stop betting.

I was asked to make a presentation at a resources conference in Winnipeg, Manitoba, and after my show, a younger fellow came up to talk to me. It turned out he was an investment advisor and a client, since he regularly bought one of the products my firm offered.

He was enthralled with a small mining company exploring and producing the specialty metal molybdenum. It became clear to me that this advisor owned an awful lot of the stock in this company personally in addition to convincing his clients to load up too. I have no idea if it worked out for him or not, but I've seen this movie over and over again. One of the worst carnal sins of any portfolio manager is falling in love with a stock. The more good news that comes out, or the higher the stock climbs, the more in love one becomes, and so every spare dollar goes towards buying more of it. And even when the stock starts going down, because the sector is losing investor interest or whatever, they keep buying. I suspected he must have bought way too much of this one, because he would talk about nothing else.

You may have been stuck golfing with a friend or visiting with a relative and they keep trying to talk you into investing in the same gold stock, biotech company, or hedge fund they own. These are symptoms of addiction. If and when the security nosedives, they are broke.

Don't bet more than you can afford to lose!

This may seem obvious to you, but let me put it another way to emphasize the message: Assume that you *are* going to lose it all, and then decide how much you want to bet. This way, you have a better understanding of what's at stake. In short:

- Gambling is okay, but it's not investing. However, the same rules that maximize the probability of acting less stupidly apply when embarking on your investment trail.
- Rely on your own judgement, not the opinion of others.
- If your investments aren't performing as you'd expect, don't panic. Think it through and act on it.
- Don't put more of your money at risk than you can afford to lose.

CHAPTER 6

DIVERSIFICATION: WANT STOCKS WITH THOSE BONDS?

After (reluctantly) departing Malibu and riding northbound, I was surprised at how truly magnificent the Pacific Coastal Highway really is. I've ridden the scenic Great Ocean Road in Australia, the Cabot Trail in Nova Scotia, the South Island of New Zealand, through the Cascade Mountains of northern Washington State, the Blue Ridge Parkway, the Sea to Sky Highway in British Columbia, and a few other roads that I'm too old to remember, but this experience was beyond words. The road was literally carved into the mountains, making it challenging to ride because of the constant switchbacks up, down, and around. One really has to pay attention, which isn't easy when every corner is like a painting you want time to study.

I was thoroughly exhausted when I finally arrived at Monterey, California. Normally I do a little search before picking a hotel to stay at. I find the reviews available on the Internet usually quite reliable. It's much easier to tell you've made a bad hotel pick than a stock or mutual fund pick. A dead giveaway is when homeless people lingering in front of the hotel outnumber the tourists. I should have hightailed it back up to the main highway where I passed a number of

hotels and motels more suited to my taste, but I was too tired and vowed to remedy things the following day.

Don't get me wrong. Although sections of the hotel were under construction and the room very small, the price was reasonable enough. It wasn't such a bad deal, but life is short. There are times when you have no choice but to just grin and bear it, like when you want to sell a stock but it's after hours and your broker is unavailable. The maverick way is to admit you made a mistake and just fix it as soon as you can. Hmm, like I should've done with that Bank of New England stock. By the way, there's a "new" Bank of New England, and it has no ties with the old one that went bankrupt.

My original plan was to avoid San Francisco—been there, done that, and there's always traffic in a big city. But to improve my spirits, a change of plan was in order. I decided I'd find a nice hotel down by Fisherman's Wharf and spend some time watching people and eating fresh seafood.

So far, this book has focused on what not to do and some important things you should know if you're going to be a maverick investor. I'm sure much of what I've presented will sound pretty scary to a novice investor. What I've done is concentrate on the equivalent of lightning strikes in real life. In reality, the odds of being hit by lighting are negligible, but if you're going to be a golfer, it's important to know that carrying around a graphite lightning rod in a thunderstorm will increase those odds a bit. Being unprepared when investing money is like carrying that graphite golf club/lightning rod during a thunderstorm.

Investing your money can be fun and rewarding as long as you are aware of the more hazardous pitfalls early on and are therefore more likely to avoid them. There are just a few more things to know before we move from "what not to do" and "what you need to know" and we begin discussing things a maverick investor "will do."

Diversification

Definition: diversification – a portfolio strategy designed to reduce exposure to risk by combining a variety of investments, such as stocks, bonds, and real estate, which are unlikely to all move in the same direction.

The industry flaunts the notion of diversification as the ideal way to mitigate volatility or risk. You now should know that volatility is not necessarily risky.

Definition: volatility – if the price of a stock moves

up and down rapidly over short periods, it has high volatility. If the price almost never changes, it has low volatility.

If it's *up* volatility, it's actually the opposite of risk, isn't it? Another important thing to know is that a badly executed effort to diversify can actually cause more volatility rather than reduce it.

I jotted this line down from an article posted on Advisor.ca on July 7, 2010, under the title "No bond bubble forming: McOuatt":

> To state the obvious, risk appetite is the first casualty of a yo-yo market. Investors take a flight to safety and bonds come back in vogue. Not surprisingly, the market volatility of the past six months has caused a continued influx of capital into fixed income.

What does this tell us? First, the cynic in me says a bubble has probably already formed or else this analyst wouldn't be in denial mode. I hope that you are beginning to *interpret* news items instead of just *reading* them. Ever since the financial crisis began, when panic first drove people into fixed income (and drove the prices for bonds up and the yields down), the asset class has attracted more and more investors. When most of your funds are in bonds, and less are in stocks or other types of assets, then you run the risk of not being diversified. Why have bonds continued to garner enthusiasm? Because interest rates have remained relatively steady.

If rates go down, the value of the bonds you hold (their

prices if you want to sell them in the market) go up. This happened a while ago already, so inflows of new money are coming from new investors buying into the past performance, hoping it will continue.

Why have interest rates (at the time of writing this book) remained low? Uncertainty is one reason. A July 26, 2001, headline from the *Los Angeles Times* reads: "Eyes turn to the danger of deflation." This reflects the current mood, which is fully reflected in bond prices today. On the very same day, the following headline appeared with much smaller print and less emphasis in the *New York Times*: "Industries find surging profits in deeper cuts." A maverick would find it intriguing that earnings reports are so positive, yet nobody seems to care. In fact, the subtitle for the same article reads: "Black ink, but doubts on sustained growth." Rising industrial profitability is great for the stock market, and when it's accompanied by "doubt," it's particularly good news for the maverick investor.

There are many historical precedents suggesting that when corporate profitability seems the most bleak, the next step is for profits to improve. Ten years ago, I had the following slide in a presentation I was making to skeptical clients. As we now know, the bottoming of profit margins occurred just before the stock market rebounded for at least a five-year uninterrupted stretch.

After reading those headlines, I would have had no problem advising (only if asked) at this exact point in time that savings be moved out of bonds and any other asset classes (REITs? bank stocks?) that are extremely sensitive to interest rates and into the stock market, which is showing

definite signs of finding its legs in the near future. Of course, behind my advice are countless hours of study and experience. I'm not sure you are ready to try this at home alone just yet.

Investors at the time of the above news items were generally less diversified than they should have been. Most of their savings were in an asset class at high risk. Why? We already discussed the perils of developing bubbles or investment "traffic jams," and it looks like there may be a bond market bubble to contend with in the later months of 2010. If corporate profitability and, by extension, the economy are improving, then eventually interest rates will rise as Main Street America begins to require capital to grow.

Interest rates generally rise for one of two reasons:

1) Government policy wants to deliberately slow the economy.

2) Demand for credit is rising in a strong economy, and if you need to borrow, you must pay a higher rate of interest.

In a strengthening economy, companies will want to borrow money and can finally afford to. They will also be willing to pay a higher rate of interest to get the funds they need. When rates do rise (and bond prices fall), the bond bubble will burst and bond owners will lose money.

When the herd decides to abandon bonds and realizes that doubts about corporate earnings weren't warranted, they will begin flowing money back into the stock market again *en masse*, causing bond prices to fall (interest rates trend higher) and stock prices to rise. Maverick investors should already own stocks and be prepared to sell them to the oncoming (stampeding?) herd at a profit when it suits them to do so.

What does any of the above have to do with diversification? It's commonly believed that if you own stocks and bonds (different "asset classes," as we call them in industry lingo), and one class does poorly, the other should do better and provide an offset, thereby reducing overall volatility.

It's necessary to bridge the gap between what you've been taught about diversification and what it really means.

Myth: Diversification reduces risk!

If only it were so simple. Let's consider a few different approaches to diversification:

Case 1

Imagine you are equally weighted with half of your money in stocks and half in bonds when the stock market crashes. Suddenly, the stocks are worth much less, no longer representing half your total savings. You decide that since bonds are performing better (which, as we've seen, they did during the years following the recent financial crisis), so why not move more of your remaining money in stocks over to bonds? If you do, you will no longer be diversified and will be overly invested in bonds. You will lose lots of your hard earned savings when bonds tank.

Case 2

Let's start again with 50% in bonds and 50% in cash. As the stock market crashes this time, you try to maintain your original diversification target of 50/50. So as the value of the bonds rise relative to stocks, you continue to sell bonds (at a profit) and buy more stocks (which are "on sale"). In my mind, this approach is vastly superior to the first case.

Case 3

Beginning again with an even split, this time when the stocks plunge in value, you sell the rising bonds at a profit and allocate even more than 50% to the depressed stock market. In this case, you are deliberately becoming less diversified by skewing your mix of assets in favour of the asset class that's declined. This is the *maverick's* approach.

Are you having trouble getting your head around this stuff? Think of your money as water in a glass, and the glass is half full. If you keep drinking a little from the glass (Case 1), you'll eventually have nothing. If whenever you take a drink you add back enough water to take it back to half full, the level in your glass never changes (Case 2). Alternatively, you may take a drink now and then, but you always add more water than you drank (Case 3) so that eventually your glass will be full.

Notice that you could apply all three strategies to a portfolio of two stocks, or two mutual funds or hedge funds, or two different exchange-traded commodity funds. In fact, you can easily have more than two asset categories—more dimensions to contend with, but essentially the same idea.

The important thing is that the different securities must behave differently at different times so that your portfolio is really diversified. It doesn't work when they move together. Refer back to the investment club I started in my university days. It turned out that all the stocks were highly sensitive to the price of oil, so they all performed badly when the oil price declined. This was terrible diversification.

Nothing is ever perfect. There are occasions when bonds and stocks move together for certain periods. These times are great if both asset classes are moving up together and you're making money hand over fist, but what to do about it is as confusing to seasoned professionals as it is for your average Joe. If they're moving up together, there's a chance they'll move down together and your diversification plans won't do what was expected.

When a variety of industry groups are moving up together, as almost always happens in a strong stock market environment, then the mission is to try to skew your stock portfolio in favour of those industries that have room to go up more than others and to underweight or avoid those that have already had their day. When stickhandling in hockey, you want to keep moving towards the goal. In the stock market, you always want to be moving into those stocks that perform better in the next stage of an economic cycle. We will get into this in more depth in the coming chapters.

From a maverick investor's perspective, improper diversification means arranging the mix of assets to minimize volatility in such a way that sacrifices the potential for decent rates of return. Many financial advisors and their employers have no problem recommending this avenue to you. With minimal volatility, you will not complain about ups and downs, and the funds will remain status quo, so your advisor's fee revenue isn't volatile either. This helps stabilize their overall business.

What does inefficient diversification look like? Whenever you're making money in one stock but losing roughly the same amount in another one, you're not getting ahead. Similarly, bonds may be performing well, but the losses in your stock holdings offset these gains and so on. If your gains are always offset by your losses, you are not making progress and are overly diversified.

Myth: Buy and hold works.

Advice such as buy and hold gives maverick investors the creeps. When it comes to investing, the exception is the rule. For example, consider the case of Nortel Networks. I was presenting at a seminar shortly after the Bell Canada spinout of their stake in Nortel. A little old lady asked me quite seriously, "I held my Bell Canada stock for more than fifteen years and until now it hasn't done much for me. Now that they've given me Nortel stock, which has been doing much better, shouldn't I sell the remaining Bell stock I own and use the money to buy more Nortel?"

For years, her Bell Canada shares provided a decent dividend, but on a total return basis, having held Bell Canada over the years provided okay but modest returns compared to, say, several of the Canadian bank stocks and many others. Everything changed suddenly when the technology/communications bubble made Nortel a sexy stock, and since Bell owned so much of it before the spinout of Nortel shares in the form of a dividend to Bell shareholders, some of that sexiness even rubbed off on Bell shares too.

What if the little old lady did switch from a buy-and-hold Bell Canada strategy to a buy-and-hold Nortel strategy? On January 14, 2009, Nortel filed for bankruptcy protection in the U.S., Canada, and the U.K. in order to restructure its debt and financial obligations. The little old lady would have lost everything.

Are you wondering what I told her in response to her query? I suggested that she sell all her Bell and Nortel. If she listened to my advice, she would have saved herself a lot of grief when the market, and particularly telecommunications stocks, crashed and burned not long after that seminar.

Given enough time, good things go bad, and given enough time, bad things sometimes get better. Buy and hold only makes sense when it's your home, and only then because you live there. It's not an investment in the conventional sense; it's much more than that.

The best example I can think of to make my point is the idea of riding along the Pacific Coastal Highway and insisting upon going in a straight line.

Trying to drive in a straight line (buy and hold) will end up in certain disaster. You will either hit a wall of solid rock head on or ride straight off a cliff. The next chapter will explain why a maverick-inspired strategy is always vastly superior to buy and hold.

San Francisco is famous for the cool summers. Each morning is overcast, but the afternoons are usually sunny; yet, the temperature remains 60°F to 70°F (about 15°C to 20°C) all day long.

The next leg of my ride, north along the coast from San

Francisco, was delightful. The temperature became 10°F to 15°F warmer an hour north along the coast. South of San Francisco, the countryside is primarily agricultural—fields filled with migrant pickers of artichokes and other vegetables and fruit. However, north of the city, the rolling hills are filled with dairy farms and cattle ranches.

Just when I thought the scenery couldn't get any better, it always would. I didn't cover many miles that day. Each little community was so quaint I'd have to stop for a coffee or a meal. While on the road, I had to take advantage of every opportunity to pull over and admire the view.

Ever since leaving Malibu, eagles were constantly soaring overhead as a reminder that we must savour freedom during every waking moment. Occasionally, an eagle would playfully fly down the mountainside above my motorcycle, almost as a welcoming gesture.

With my throttle hand getting sore, my left leg stiff from having to continually shift gears, and the temperature getting much cooler as evening drew near, I decided to stop for the night at a lovely inn with an ocean view in the village of Mendocino.

It was quite a coincidence. When touring, there's not much time to turn on the television, but when I had switched it on back in downtown Monterey, a government official from Mendocino County was being interviewed on a local news channel. He said he was embarrassed about 60% of the county's economy being dependent one way or another on the marijuana trade.

Here I was settled down for the evening in Mendocino, and I couldn't help but wonder if this official had ever been to Pennsylvania to see what happens when the coal mines shut down or to a northern Canadian town where the lumber mill had been mothballed. If he had, I'm sure he'd be blessing the thriving drug trade that is clearly paying his salary, rather than being "embarrassed" by it.

Research or Cognitive Dissonance

> *Definition: Cognitive dissonance is a psychological phenomenon that refers to the discomfort felt at a discrepancy between what you already know or believe and new information or interpretation.*

Before moving on to discussing what a maverick investor does, it's necessary to know what investment research is all about. There are many extremely capable financial analysts working in the subsidiary investment dealer operations of banks, independent brokerage firms, and asset or fund management companies. I mentioned earlier that if you can get your hands on published research, whether it is big picture stuff (economic or strategic analysis) or information on particular industries or stocks, then you should use it, but ignore the recommendations.

The work an analyst does well, understanding and explaining to others complex economic and business relationships and their impact on financial data, is valuable (whether it's measuring increasing unemployment for big picture stuff or earnings for a company), but most good analysts would be far happier doing the research and never having to make a recommendation. This is the Peter Principle hard at work, which states that "in a hierarchy, every employee tends to rise to his or her level of incompetence."

To earn promotions and more income, an analyst must make recommendations, but being a researcher doesn't train you to offer advice. Research requires a data-hungry detail-oriented bulldog, while making recommendations requires a decision maker willing to take great personal risk. Over the years, I've known a few analysts who decided to set up their own pure research businesses in order to escape the pressure of having to add "buy, sell, or hold" advice to their reports.

Although the research is straightforward, there are few investment firms that won't demand that recommendations be vetted by senior managers and compliance personnel. It's impossible for any group (with the possible exception of a few cowboys working on a ranch) to think in tandem like mavericks. The group is riddled with behavioural conflict and is motivated to make decisions that minimize personal and corporate risk.

I was making a speech to an accounting association many years ago. To make a point, I had two research reports about the same biotech company with me. The same major U.S. investment firm published them three days apart. One report was a buy recommendation and the other report was a sell recommendation. I could sense their disbelief, so I passed both reports around the room so the accountants could confirm I wasn't exaggerating. Accountants are like that, you know, hungering for proof.

How could this be? I knew the analyst personally, and it was unlikely he would have changed his opinion overnight. It turns out the firm had changed their big picture outlook based on a rapid deterioration in the market on one day, so all buy recommendations were reversed the following day.

People make decisions and become very uncomfortable when they receive new information that contradicts or makes the decision questionable. The psychological term for the phenomenon is *cognitive dissonance*, but I believe the discomfort stems from uncertainty and risk mixed together.

Every decision involves risk. There's no need to belabour that point, is there? It's easier to make decisions when there seems to be less uncertainty about the outcome. This is why buy recommendations are made long after the stock has gone up. The fact that the stock price is rising confirms that other people are buying it, so a buy recommendation feels less risky.

The reverse is also true. There aren't many sell recommendations out there, since the analyst's ability to do research on a company at all will be threatened if he angers the company's management. A sell recommendation will surely not be received warmly. We all believe that investment analysts should be able to express their opinions openly without the threat of retaliation by company management, but this is a pipedream.

Once upon a time, a fellow portfolio manager was doing a TV spot, and a caller asked him about a small technology company that sold an inexpensive software application that was supposedly easy to install and use. Candidly, my associate explained that he had actually gone out and bought the software this company was selling, but after spending many hours trying to get it to work, he gave up.

No sooner than when he was back in the office, sitting at his desk, the phone began ringing. The president of the company threatened legal action and insisted that the software would work fine if he were to send a technician to help. My friend's retort was, "If I need a technician, then it is hardly easy to use."

Once an analyst is chastised for making a negative recommendation, you can be sure they will be reluctant to do it again. However, if the stock has really been hammered in the market already, then the analyst will feel compelled to make a sell recommendation or at least reduce it to a hold recommendation by peer pressure within the firm. Since there are obviously sellers out there driving down the price of the stock anyway, the analyst's personal risk would be lower. An analyst will feel more comfortable with a sell recommendation or with reducing a recommendation from a buy to a hold if they aren't the only one doing it.

Professional money managers have the advantage of being inundated with published research from a wide variety of sources. Over time, it is possible to get a feel for patterns in recommendations and use them to your advantage. I remember long ago that whenever the investment firm Smith Barney (before it was acquired by Morgan Stanley) would publish a buy recommendation, I'd immediately sell the stock if I owned it. It worked like clockwork. Soon after their buy report was published, the stock would plummet. Bad advice that is consistently wrong can be useful—a maverick just does the opposite.

There are a select few maverick analysts out there who are bullheaded and will only publish what they really think, but they're difficult for a professional to find and virtually impossible to find for someone investing from home. Your investment advisor may be familiar with one in the firm, so don't be afraid to ask.

Just to demonstrate how convoluted a research report can be, I found an undated clip from an old report I must have subconsciously saved just to share with you. I can't recall (better that I can't for liability reasons) which brokerage firm published it, but I'm pretty sure you'll find it as confusing and amusing as I did.

> **Abitibi Consolidated Inc.** (A C$4.85, TSX/ABY US$4.31, NSYE) **Rating Buy—Above-Average Risk, Target C$5.50**
>
> - 1Q06 results were not as strong as anticipated but showed improvement in key segments.
> - In the months ahead, product price momentum should be perceptible in both the newsprint and commercial printing divisions.
> - Market perception appears to be turning positive despite further strengthening of the Canadian dollar; maintaining buy rating and C$5.50 target.
>
> Abitibi reported Q1 EPS from continuing operations of -$0.10 compared to the mean of -$0.07 and our forecast of -$0.03. We attribute the shortfall to higher-than-anticipated costs. Alternatively viewed, the cost reductions are not materializing as rapidly as expected. The impact is negative, and we are lowering our twelve-month target to $5.75/share from $6.00/share.
>
> Given the high operating rates, we expect a steady increase in newsprint pricing. Our twelve-month target is based on a 2007E projected P/E multiple of 13x and EV/EBITDA multiple of 5.3x.

Let me summarize. Despite the fact that the results are improving, and market perception has turned positive for the stock, the loss was slightly worse than the analyst expected, so his reading of the earnings report is negative and he's therefore lowering his target price. Oh, and by the way, the stock is still rated a buy. Is this confusing you? Me too!

For fun, I've reproduced below an e-mail I wrote and sent to a few thousand of my advisor clients. It's undated but will provide a flavour for how a maverick investor might analyze the same forest products sector.

> You might recall last year that a few of the business papers quoted me about forest products. No doubt, the journalists noticed a significant weighting in Mavrix Explorer Fund (the resources mutual fund I launched and was managing) and considered it so "out there" that they couldn't resist publishing it.
>
> At the time I was interviewed for the article, I pointed out that since nobody owned the stocks (especially institutional fund managers, since retail investors never own them), the risk of a sell off was remote. All the news was (and is) negative. The only bright spot was the return of duties collected by the U.S. prior to the new Softwood Lumber Agreement. For example, here's a summary from a research report I just received:
>
> - Newsprint – consumption drop accelerating so far in 2007
> - Pulp – February price increase postponed to April, but softwood remains tight

- Printing & Writing – Demand remains weak; supply side response coming
- Wood products – Not much light at the end of the tunnel

The point is that fundamentals can be important, but oftentimes it's the supply/demand balance of the stocks that can be the more important factor. Look at the performance of the following stocks since the beginning of the year despite all that doom and gloom:

	16-Apr-07	1-Dec-07	Return
Canfor (CFP)	$10.26	$12.44	21.25%
Interfor (IFP.A)	$7.00	$8.88	26.86%
Abitibi (A)	$2.65	$3.40	28.30%
West Fraser (WFT)	$42.00	$43.76	4.19%
Domtar (UFS)	$8.19	$11.27	37.61%
Group Average			23.64%
S&P/TSX Comp	12,754.75	13,659.98	7.10%

Nothing has changed fundamentally for these stocks, so why have they performed so well? As I mentioned, the downside was (is) limited: no sellers. Also, with a number of large cap stocks disappearing from the Canadian market, the weight devoted to other sectors will necessarily increase in institutional portfolios provided the weight in Canadian equities remains constant (i.e. they will be buyers). The improvement in balance sheets due to the softwood duty refunds increases the likelihood of consolidation and restructuring in the industry (buyers). The point of my bringing this stuff up is simply to highlight what you and I already know but sometimes forget. Returns don't always stem from poring over current data—information everybody has access to. Often enough, all you have to do is think about what has to happen in the future. It can be a painful wait, but if it "has to happen," then the probability of your being right eventually is very high.

> Reading through some quantitative research, I can't help but notice that profit margins in sectors such as telecom, media and technology, health care, and consumer staples are *booming*. We can find many examples of stocks in these categories where there aren't many sellers. Meanwhile, the attention of the media and published research is still focused on materials, resources, and cyclicals. It doesn't take a brain surgeon to figure out which way the funds will eventually flow.

Here's a more current update on a forest products stock from an analyst I know well. He's always a "sitting on the fence" kind of guy, so I would be surprised if his "market perform" rating will ever change. Here's an excerpt from the report:

> Canfor reported Q2/10 EPS from continuing operations of $0.20 compared to the first call mean of $0.15 and our estimate of $0.13. We attribute the outperformance to higher lumber prices and lower sawmill conversion costs. We expect a drop in earnings in

Q3/10 due to the weak U.S. housing market and lower profits at Canfor Pulp due to discounting in pulp.

Most reports read like this one when the company is doing notably better than the analyst predicted. But if lumber prices were higher, why wasn't it reflected in his estimates? Why would he expect a drop in earnings due to the weak housing market? The U.S. housing market has been weak for more than five years running at the time I'm writing this book, yet earnings still came in better than expected. I could go on, but the point is the conflicting messages are because of *cognitive dissonance.* The analyst is in a box. He must justify his recommendation despite evidence that's arisen to the contrary.

The maverick investor is only interested in the fact that things are looking brighter for the industry and the company, and best of all, nobody seems to care. While the press and the herd focus on sexy gold stocks for example (see chart below), there are at least a dozen other industries poised to perform well.

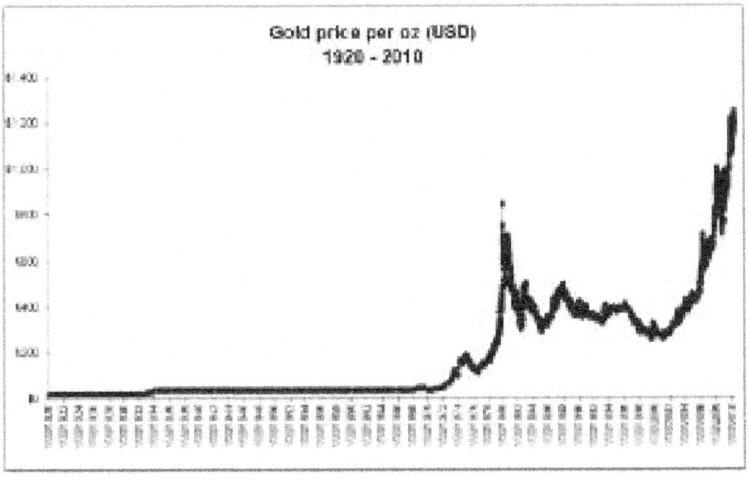

Considering where gold prices are relative to the past, it's not surprising that the herd is jamming to get into gold stocks around the time of writing this book. Reading the newspapers and blogs out there, you'd think there weren't any other sectors out there performing well enough to deserve investor attention.

Consider the following clip posted July 27, 2010, on Tech Talk on the website Timing the Market:

> **U.S. equity index futures are higher this morning.** S&P 500 futures are up 7 points in pre-opening trade. Strength can be attributed to a series of second quarter reports that exceeded consensus earnings estimates and included positive third quarter guidance. Companies in this category include AK Steel, Dupont, UBS, Daimler, Lockheed Martin, Lexmark, Domino's Pizza, Rogers Communications, Cummins, Office Depot....

Tunnel vision is a herd phenomenon. While the herd is (as always) obsessing about one or a few industry sectors and corresponding stocks, the maverick investor is open to any company, industry, or fund that will make money. If companies are reporting earnings better than expected, the stocks are or will be going higher.

PART THREE

WHAT A MAVERICK INVESTOR DOES

CHAPTER 7

GOING IT ALONE OR USING A TRAIL GUIDE: MUTUAL FUNDS CAN BE FUN

Out of the several thousand investment advisors and financial planners I've met over the years, there are several hundred who have maverick instincts. If you don't mind using a trail guide, then I strongly recommend you find one who has views compatible with those you've been reading about.

I was looking to hire a new sales rep for my company and received a resumé from a fellow who was actually an investment advisor looking for a change. He believed selling mutual funds would be less stressful. I arranged to meet with him.

I happened to be standing on the street in front of the building when this black BMW pulls up and a jittery youngster (young compared to me anyway) gets out. He was wearing an expensive suit and had his hair gelled straight back like Gordon Gekko's, the fictional big-swinging dick from the movie *Wall Street*, portrayed brilliantly by Michael Douglas. At work, I was usually dressed in jeans and a Harley-Davidson T-shirt and was never surprised when visitors walked right on by me, without even a nod, to go up to the office for a meeting with the CEO (which would be me).

I didn't hire him. A fellow maverick is not into role-playing. If the advisor you're thinking of working with looks a lot like this fellow, then I'd think twice. It is okay, I suppose, to have a nice car and to dress nicely, but a "look at me" aura is a warning sign. When someone deliberately adorns the trappings of success, I believe there's insecurity in their personality. Mavericks reek of confidence but don't need or want to stand out from the crowd by adorning themselves with accoutrements.

You must be realistic. Your advisor does work for a financial services firm, so any evidence that they are willing to deviate from the party line is a good signal. Ask them what they think about the market or a mutual fund, or even an individual stock or two. If they simply regurgitate the newspaper headlines or are in love with a top performing mutual fund ("you can't eat past performance" is one of my favourite expressions), or their favourite stocks are everyone else's favourite stocks too, find another advisor. On the other hand, if you sense a real independent thinker willing to disagree with conventional wisdom, this advisor is a keeper.

Think of your investments as a tree. If the conditions are good—the nutrients in the soil are nourishing, there's enough sunlight, and the moisture is just right—then just like the giant redwood trees along the northern California coastline, your savings will slowly but surely grow big.

A maverick investor knows there's no "big score" that will happen overnight. By methodically and consistently adhering to a common sense approach, you will surely reach your goals.

Mutual Funds or Fun?

Usually the first vehicle of choice for new investors on the investment highway is a mutual fund. Since it's usually an equity fund, or a fund investing in the stock market, we'll focus on these and talk about bond and money market funds later.

Oftentimes, the first mutual fund experience is a disappointing one. There's a reason for this. People intuitively want to be associated with success, so their first mutual fund will have these characteristics:

- A great track record of top quartile performance over at least three to five years.
- Billions of dollars invested in it, so it's "safe."
- Offered by an investment firm with a long and "distinguished" history.

A maverick takes nothing for granted. Many years ago, there was much less data readily available and few statistical tools at one's disposal. (I was around when the first spreadsheets appeared, and they weren't very friendly to work with.) I was curious and decided to examine a group of funds over time to see what their performance looked like. Below is a slide I dug up from a presentation I made sharing the results:

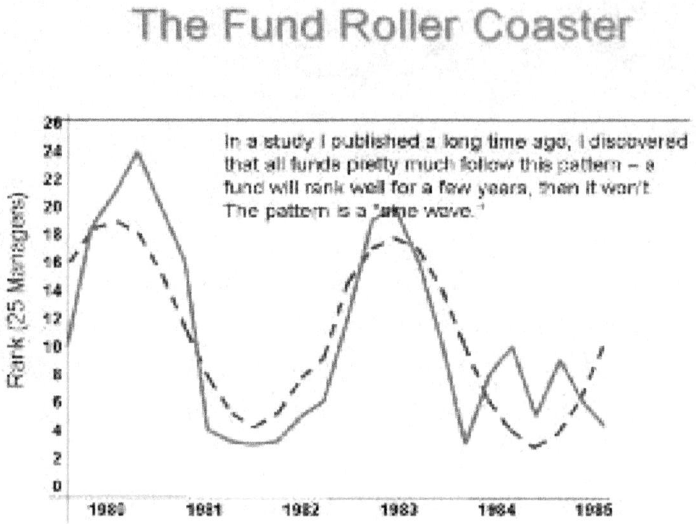

I don't want to frighten you if you're not mathematically inclined, but I managed to statistically "fit" every fund in the sample into a sine function. A sine function is simply a wave like the one in the diagram. The wave goes up awhile, then down awhile in a predictable fashion. The graph is one of the funds in my study and how it ranked over time. The left axis is where the fund ranks—in this case, it is among the top performing funds when it ranks #3 or #4 in a sample of thirty funds. If it ranks #24, it's a dog.

It doesn't take a mathematician to interpret a picture. If you invest in the fund when it's a dog, the odds are great that it will be a top performer soon enough. The problem is that most investors will pick a top performer, often with the help of their advisor, who is just human and knows it's easier to get you to buy into a good performer than a bad one. However, the top performer will soon become a dog, and the investor will be unhappy.

A great track record might actually guarantee poor performance.

When it comes to your money, intuition sucks. You "intuitively" steer towards something that "feels good." A maverick must strip out the emotional baggage and do what seems right rationally.

There is enough publicly available data nowadays to help you find a few funds that suit your tastes and examine their performance patterns. What suits your tastes may include funds that are easy to buy in and out of, whose comments you have read in the press, whose portfolio manager sounds smart on TV, or that are socially responsible funds. When one of the funds does occasionally perform very well but has been in a slump over the past year or two, buy it. After the performance has improved over the course of a couple of years and you're happy with the results, sell it and buy a different fund that is in a slump.

More recently, I had the urge to see if award-winning funds followed the same pattern. After all, if someone wants a top-performing fund, wouldn't they head straight for the ones that have just won awards for their outstanding performance? I shared the results of my study in an e-mail to my clients, which is reproduced below:

> As an exercise, we looked at the award-winning funds since 2002 and how their performance looked the next year. Rather than examine every category (overkill), we stuck to basic Canadian equity, U.S. equity, small cap, international equity, and bond categories and included the "thematic" funds at the time, such as precious metals more recently and dividend and income category funds.
>
> Results:
>
> - In 2002, 100% of the winners were either 1st or 2nd quartile funds. The next year, 88% of these had fallen to 3rd or 4th quartile.
> - In 2003, only 40% of winners were 1st quartile funds. All the 3rd quartile funds rose to 1st quartile in the following year.
> - In 2004, 86% of the winners were 1st and 2nd quartile funds. The next year only 43% were 1st quartile and 2nd quartile, and 43% were 3rd and 4th quartile (flip a coin).
> - In 2005, 100% of winners were either 1st or 2nd quartile. The following year, 70% were still 1st and 2nd quartile—most of the good stayed good....but a fluke?
> - In 2006, 67% were 1st and 2nd quartile funds, but the next year, 83% had drifted to 3rd and 4th quartile.

> Bottom line: Winning an award (being a top performer) is not an indication of what happens, even in the following year. In fact, the odds are awfully good that your 1st or 2nd quartile pick will be below the median or worse one year later. Interesting! If there's a lesson, I suppose it's simply that funds should be bought because they meet your objectives, not because they've been performing well recently.

It's not important to understand why this roller coaster occurs for all equity mutual funds, it just does. Markets change, so, for example, when a growth fund invested primarily in technology stocks suffers, it's no doubt because the upward trend in technology stocks, or their popularity among the herd, has either stopped or deteriorated. Many portfolio managers, lots of them friends of mine, lost their jobs when the technology bubble burst.

Portfolio managers are just people working for people. I've been subjected to the following scenario and have watched it occur time and again:

- Fund performance begins to soar.
- Fund attracts lots of new money.
- Marketing folks want more and more time from portfolio manager for meetings.
- Money pours into the fund in droves.
- Portfolio manager's head swells (the "I'm a genius" syndrome).
- Performance begins to deteriorate.
- Money leaves the fund in droves.
- Portfolio manager has to sell the fund's best stocks (there are still buyers for these).

- Performance sucks, and it takes two to three years for things to get back to normal.

Size just doesn't matter.

A thinking person should be able to figure out that it doesn't take a big fund or a big fund company to provide good performing funds. Think about it. Do you shop at the big box stores because the level of service is better? Is the quality of the merchandise better? No. You shop there because the economy of scale for the store allows them to buy products at a lower cost. They can order in bigger volumes and squeeze their suppliers. They then pass these savings to their customers.

For reasons I don't understand, the larger financial institutions have managed to convince the investing public that similar economies of scale exist when it comes to investing your money. Of course, the transactions and administration costs of the bank or insurance company are lower, and perhaps some of these benefits might come your way in the form of lower fees (excuse me, I'm "laughing out loud," as the kids say) and expenses, but we're not talking about buying lawnmowers. Rates of return on funds managed nimbly and intelligently make those fees and expenses pale by comparison.

I'm not planning to provide a lesson in what "management expense ratios" mean because they just don't matter. The business press and consultants who've never managed money invented them and are not maverick-inclined, and these types of "cost-centric" stats are popular with the big players in the industry because it helps them justify their own grandiosity.

Bigger is safer possibly when you're banking, but legitimate capital management companies are structured so that they never really touch your money. The custodial (where the money is physically held) and administrative (record-keeping) functions are usually provided by banks or huge financial institutions anyway—for safety and regulatory reasons and to make the potential for fraud near impossible—and are provided to asset management companies at modest cost.

The reason why large financial services companies got into the fund management business was simply economics. They were providing banking, custodial, and administrative services to mutual fund and other asset management companies anyway, so why not also earn management fees by offering their own mutual funds and private wealth management services? More profit for their firm.

Take it from someone who knows from experience. Managing a massive quantity of money in one fund is much more difficult for a portfolio manager. You can only buy big companies. A portfolio manager will try to buy the best big companies, but since everyone else with big portfolios is doing the same thing, it's not like you can outsmart them. It's sort of like playing poker with jacks, queens, and kings being the only cards in the deck. If the three other players see three kings on the table, everyone knows there's still one in someone's hand.

It's not nearly as easy to sell or buy stocks in the market as people think, and we've discussed this previously. Sometimes you can't sell any stocks at all during a market crisis, and if some really bad news comes out about a company, you won't be easily selling its stock either.

Trying to sell a big stock position requires a big buyer who won't necessarily be there when most needed. Besides, as soon as you place your sell order with a broker, the whole world knows a big stock position is for sale and the price of the stock will fall immediately. There is a large segment of the industry that makes money selling borrowed stock (which is called short selling) when they see a really big seller out there. These folks know the price will fall, so they sell stock they don't even own and buy it back later at a lower price than they sold it at, thereby making a profit. This should be illegal in my opinion, but it isn't. Imagine the trouble you'd be in if you sold a house you didn't own?

Large portfolios are more economical for the large financial companies, not the client. They can buy services they require (communications infrastructure, computer hardware and software, stock and bond quotations, news services and advertising space, etc.) in bulk and reduce their expenses. Should there be good performance in a handful of the hundreds of funds they offer, which will happen periodically, even by accident, it is just a bonus for the big investment firms, since they can promote the heck out of the good performance to attract new customers and generate more fees and revenues.

It's a small world after all.

You will be better served from an investment performance perspective, as well as the level of service you will get, if you concentrate your efforts, or instruct your advisor accordingly, on finding smaller fund companies where the objectives of the portfolio managers is aligned with your own.

All professional money managers, when not motivated by an employer to do otherwise, will focus on being careful but creative with your money. The difference isn't subtle—they want to impress you and their peers by getting you spectacular investment results; minimizing their own operating expenses is a secondary matter. When not forced into buying big household stocks such as IBM, Proctor & Gamble, U.S. Steel, and the like, they will delight in finding, researching, and trading less widely known companies, and buying them smart and selling them smart too. Over many years, I've noticed that when equity mutual fund returns are in the double digits (20% or 30% over two- and three-year periods), nobody gives a hoot about the 2% or even 3% management expense ratio for the funds.

I'm reminded of my younger days. I was invited many times to go to New York and participate in the *Wall Street Transcript* Roundtable, where portfolio manager types from around the United States (and one lonely Canadian guy) would chat about their opinions concerning the economy, financial markets, and their favourite stock picks. They would then publish the transcript of these discussions in their widely read (among investors anyway) periodical.

Every time I'd fly down to participate, I would be surprised that the stock picks from these gurus were always the largest publicly traded companies, and they almost never recommended any interesting smaller (not *small* mind you, just *smaller*) but faster growing companies. And hardly ever did these portfolio managers *dislike* any stocks. It wasn't until many years later that I realized they managed *really big* portfolios, and so were pretty much confined to owning big companies. You might as well like the stocks you owned, because selling them would be too difficult.

Before moving along to different styles of equity funds, it's worth mentioning that in a marketing-driven financial services firm (keep bringing in new money, keep operating expenses low), there is a need to keep introducing new products. It's not really much different from the proliferation of new mobile phones with "enhanced" features every few months. The only difference is the "new features" for investment funds aren't contributing to performance, so they need to sound sexy. This is why you'll always see announcements like this:

> **NEW: Multi-style all-cap equity fund launches**
> New fund benefits from the expertise of [insert name of any financial firm here].

The new fund, of course, is managed by the same team of professionals managing an already available fund and has a marketing and rollout budget of many millions of dollars. I can promise you the *past* performance (which any buyer of the new fund won't get…it is *past*) of the already available fund must be good, or they wouldn't be flaunting the same "expertise." The already available fund (or funds) clearly isn't growing fast enough, so they launch a clone of sorts, or a new fund that invests in the other fund (or funds), with lots of hype and hoopla, and they attract more assets, more fees, and more revenues. It's a business.

With thousands of mutual funds and hedge funds already out there that have publicly available performance histories and characteristics that can be analyzed, why would you need to jump at the chance to buy a new one? A maverick investor knows better.

Value or Growth, or Both?

There are many styles of road to choose from on a bike tour. I enjoyed the transition from coastal mountain road to the Redwood Highway as I travelled further north along the California coastline. Beautiful and, no doubt, *ancient* trees lined the serpentine roadway as it twisted and turned through the rugged mountains. One scenic route was aptly named the Avenue of the Giants.

I rode as far as Crescent City, California, before deciding to stop for the night. Every morning so far was both cooler (50°F to 60°F, or about 10°C to 15°C) and very foggy. The fog wouldn't usually lift until early afternoon. This "style" of riding was beginning to get tiring. Having had enough of the fog and having to don a sweater, jacket, and gloves every morning, I checked the weather fifty miles in from the coastline and discovered I had been riding parallel to a sunny 80°F to 90°F (27°C to 32°C) stretch of blue skies. It was time to adopt a new style of riding.

From Crescent City, I rode along a lovely road, Highway 199, weaving through the increasingly evergreen-covered mountains towards Medford, Oregon, located in the Rogue River Valley. Once I hit the Interstate, which was much straighter, but not too straight to be boring, I could motor along at much faster speeds. Off came the extra clothing, and the change in style was well worth my while in terms of personal gratification.

About twenty years ago, I'd say, the industry and the academic community, in an effort to better understand what causes good versus bad rates of return in stock markets, began studying differing styles of investment management.

There isn't a hope of my staying awake long enough to cover even a sampling of the variety of styles that are out there, so I'll keep it simple. Two styles in particular get plenty of attention: growth and value.

With the growth style, portfolio managers use their ingenuity to identify companies that are growing most rapidly. Since I carry around a BlackBerry (aka CrackBerry), I'll use its creator Research in Motion (RIM) as an example. When the company was first getting its legs, it offered me and other research analysts a free trial of a little device with a monochrome screen that allowed you to send and receive text messages. We became addicted to them overnight and believed that this kind of service would catch on. Early movers can grow businesses very quickly with sufficient research depth, management expertise, and capital. We provided the capital to RIM and the rest is history.

Early on, RIM was a growth company because even though they weren't profitable and wouldn't be making money for many years, the company kept selling more and more units. Revenues grew like crazy and, with some occasional disruptions (a market crisis, the technology bubble bursting), so did the stock price.

Portfolio managers who specialize in companies such as RIM are commonly called "growth managers." The funds they manage are "growth funds." The portfolio will usually have many stocks in various industries. They can be fast growing companies in slow growth industries or companies benefitting from an industry that is suddenly growing. Growth stocks can be very expensive. Investors expect the company to grow fast and so are willing to pay a higher price. However, you'll have to buy a book explaining price/earnings (P/E) ratios, P/E to growth rate ratios, and price/sales (P/S) ratios if you really want to get into security analysis yourself.

A value manager is more interested in buying and owning cheap stocks. Some companies grow slowly but pay their shareowners high dividends as compensation. A stock can be in an industry that is out of favour with the investment herd, or an industry can be out of favour entirely, making all the stocks in the sector cheaper. There are measures such as price/book ratios (P/B) and price to net asset value ratios that analysts use to gauge whether or not a stock is cheap.

Growth funds are considered riskier or more volatile than value funds. For instance, if the market is going higher because of a particularly strong economy, then the growth fund should go even higher still. A value manager might not perform as well as a growth manager in a bull market but won't do as poorly in a bear market. A value manager is therefore considered more conservative.

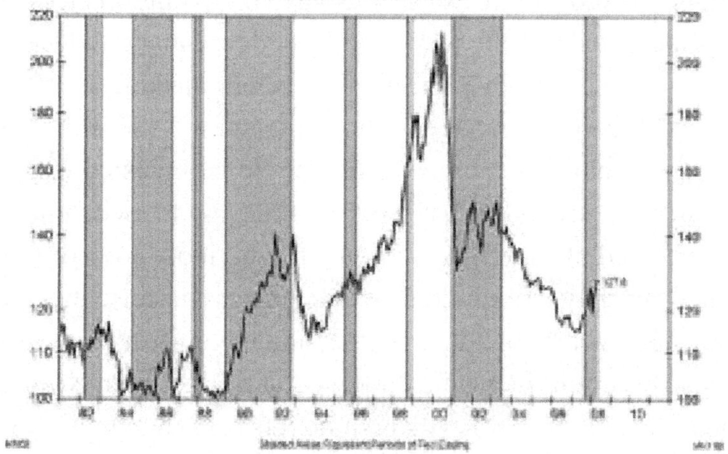

The graph above shows the relative performance of growth stocks versus value stocks in the S&P 500 Index over many years. When the line is rising, growth stocks are performing much better than value stocks. When the line is falling, value stocks are doing better. The chart is not current but makes the point well enough.

Conventional wisdom says that conservative investors who can't stomach as much volatility should use value funds and that investors who don't mind a wild ride should use growth funds. Alternatively, you can invest most of your money into a value fund while also putting some into a growth fund so that you might occasionally get more returns in a buoyant market with at least a portion of your savings.

Why not growth when growth is performing and value at other times?

There are portfolio managers like me who hate being pigeonholed into either one of these styles. However, it is inevitable that one label or the other will be associated with a money manager because of the way consulting services are compensated and the way mutual funds are marketed (when growth is sexy, they promote the growth manager).

A maverick investor who understands the ebbs and flows of market sentiment will want to be invested in their favourite growth fund at the right time and to switch into a value fund at other times. Don't forget, most advisors and the firms they work for, and even the press because they just don't know any better, will discourage you from even trying. You might be particularly bad at timing your switches and blame them for letting you do it. This is a potential risk to their reputation (and has legal implications should you really be the vindictive sort). What's worse is that you might shrink your assets, which reduces their fees and revenue forecasts.

Before you start believing I'm critical of investment firms and fees, I surely am not. The only reason we fund managers can make a living is *because* of fee revenues, and every fee or commission you pay your advisor is earned. The vast majority of people need a trail guide and shouldn't whine about having to pay for one. If your advisor loses your money at any point in time, rest assured you probably would have done much worse if you were left to your own devices.

More precisely, I am less tolerant when the culture of a financial services organization has maximizing fees as the Prime Directive (from the *Star Trek* universe, meaning a directive that takes precedence over any and all other considerations). The mission of the organization should be to provide you, the client, with the best possible investment performance consistent with your tolerance for risk and a decent level of service.

Whenever I've recommended a more active approach to selecting mutual funds in print or on television, such as using a growth fund and switching into a value fund when appropriate, I always get the same question: "How do you know when to switch?" There is an easy answer, but nobody likes hearing it. The answer is: "You will know!" If you are learning some maverick traits, then it should be obvious. You should switch when your intuition or emotions tell you not too. It's that simple. If the fund you own has been doing extremely well and drifted up towards the top quartile or is now in the "best performing funds" category (rankings are available from a wide variety of publicly available services) and so you've begun to love it dearly, it's time to switch into a different style of fund.

I shouldn't have to remind you, but a maverick investor doesn't react to ads that state things such as: "Has your fund been up 85% of the time?" There is absolutely no information of any use in this tag line. Any fund can be up 85% of the time and perform badly compared to the overall market or all of the other funds out there. Don't be lured by the creative and often misleading use of statistics. Advertisements like this are designed to put a product in your face—you are being sold to. If you want to invest in good funds, it's better to go looking for them yourself.

Bond and Money Market Funds

The northern portion of the California coast and the coastline of Oregon north to the Canadian border are often referred to as the "lost" or "forgotten" coast. It's a bit out of the way for most travellers, and the climate is certainly unpredictable.

Bond funds too are kind of lost and forgotten. Strangely, most of an investor's money ends up in bonds, either in a standalone bond fund or as part of balanced funds, which invest in both stocks and bonds, in addition to short-term securities (commonly referred to as "money market"), as a form of diversifying risk. Think of a bond as a puttering scooter and stocks as exciting choppers and sport bikes. The scooter does the job of getting you there, but there's seldom a crowd of people around it oohing and aahing over it and going on about how cool it is.

Bond managers have a tendency to avoid any sort of risk if they can help it. Unless it's a highflying high-yield specialty bond fund and positioned as such, the bond fund you're likely to use will be virtually the same as any other bond fund. The fund measurement services rank the performance histories of various bond funds as well, but on closer inspection, you will generally find the top-performing fund's rate of return isn't dramatically better than the bottom performer.

I happened across a newspaper article that listed the top consistent performing Canadian bond funds, and the numbers for the five-year annual performance ranged from a high of 8.01% to a low of 5.25%. If you consider that differing management fees can account for as much as 1% of the difference, and factor in how sensitive these numbers are to the "endpoint" (more about this in Chapter 11), it's not such a big spread.

As a conservative lot, bond managers don't like to be too different from the overall bond market in terms of riskiness, so they usually have a large position in higher quality government-guaranteed bonds with a splash of higher yielding good quality corporate bonds to add more yield.

One bond fund is usually as good as another;
any money market fund will do.

Money market funds have had a difficult time of late. The interest rate environment during the financial crisis has meant that the low (sometimes zero) rate of interest the fund is earning invested in short-term securities (such as government T-bills, asset-backed commercial paper, and so forth) was so low that it wasn't even enough to cover the funds' operating expenses. When the economy is struggling, governments will typically drop the short-term cost of borrowing money (i.e. interest rates) to help consumers and businesses recover. There have been very few times when it was necessary for central banks to drop rates to zero in order to do this, but we suffered through one of them not long ago.

If you're thinking that money market funds will be a better investment than bonds when rates start rising (when rates go up, bond prices go down), then you're really beginning to think like a maverick investor.

Balanced Funds—All You Need in One Basket?

A balanced, or diversified, fund conventionally would invest a percentage in domestic and perhaps international stocks, a percentage in bonds, and usually a small portion in short-term securities. There are some balanced funds that purport to be "tactical asset allocation funds," which use some formula or another to aggressively adjust the mix between the asset classes (stocks versus bonds versus cash) in order to enhance returns. For example:

- If interest rates are rising and hurting bond prices, have a bigger weighting in stocks.
- If the economy is floundering and stock prices falling, own more bonds.
- If both stocks and bonds are doing poorly, own more short-term securities.

My experience has been that most models used to decide which asset class to overweight fall short of the mark. This is because they involve efforts to forecast market behaviour, and profound changes in markets are always ignited by an event that couldn't have easily been predicted. The odd strategist who correctly forecasts one of these major crises is usually right only the one time, and warnings from maverick investors who are getting nervous based on headlines or other evidence of a bubble or traffic jam about to happen are largely ignored.

If an asset allocation fund is performing marvellously for some time, assume that the portfolio managers are so busy patting one another on the back and promoting their brilliance to new clients that they won't act quickly enough on any quantitative signals the model spits out warning that a change in mix is necessary. At one time, I was responsible for maintaining a similar model for one of my institutional clients and frankly became frustrated because neither the client nor any of my associates would ever take the model's asset mix recommendations seriously.

I published an obscure article entitled "Of Bulls, Bears and Wolves" long ago based on a study I conducted of the real-life asset mix decisions of a sample of pension fund investment managers. When stocks prices went up, so did their weighting in stocks. When stock prices generally moved down, so did their weighting in stocks. In other words, there weren't any real asset-mix decisions being made at all. The markets were determining the asset mix. I vaguely remember a pension consultant asking permission to reference my article in a speech she was making at a conference. Most probably her audience (pension funds) didn't like these results, which was good for her: she worked for a pension consulting firm that was hoping to earn a fee for providing asset-mix consulting services to pension plan sponsors.

Making Your Own Trail Mix

Believe it or not, there are advisors who suggest investing in a few different balanced funds. They think that if one fund manager gets it wrong, maybe another one will get the mix right. Call me crazy, but diversification to nullify risk isn't the objective; making money with your money is the objective. Upside risk is what we're after. If the performance of different funds will cancel one another out (one good + one bad = middle of the road), what's the point?

It's possible for you or your advisor to select two or more stock or equity funds that have different styles and move money on occasion from one to another in an intelligent fashion as discussed earlier. You can also add a bond and money market fund into the mix. When your maverick senses begin to tell you—based on information you are reading, headlines, or whatever you find works for you—that the tide has risen too high for the stock market, then move a significant amount of savings out of all equity funds into bonds and short term.

If you are lucky enough to find a balanced fund manager who can demonstrably and reliably accomplish this some of the time, then own that one fund and consider yourself fortunate.

CHAPTER 8

INVESTING OR PLAYING THE STOCK MARKET?

I decided to bed down in Medford, Oregon, located in the Rogue Valley for a few days. While surfing the Net in my room the first night, I happened across the website of a local bike builder whose shop has a great name: Thunder Struck. I can be a bit impulsive at times (okay, all the time) and decided to have the proprietors of the shop order me some new custom wheels for my bike. It gave me a dandy reason to hang around the quiet town for a few days.

I studied the area a bit. The Rogue Valley has been inhabited for over 8,500 years. The first non-Native Americans to arrive were the fur trappers working for the Hudson's Bay Company. This link to my country's history (the Hudson's Bay Company virtually built Canada) made me curious. Apparently, when the settlers came, there were frequent skirmishes with Native Americans in the area, until ultimately the Native Americans were relocated (a familiar story).

The town of Medford was founded around 1883, when a group of railroad surveyors decided this would be the best route to run the Oregon and California railroad through the Valley. Coincidentally, I had dinner the evening before at one of the train stations, which is more than one hundred years old and has been refurbished into a dining establishment that serves up a fine rib eye.

I was itching for a day trip, with no pressure of having to get somewhere, and began riding from my hotel at 1,428 feet above sea level through the Cascades Mountains along the winding and scenic road adjacent to the Rogue River. The river is well known for its fine salmon runs. I learned there have been plenty of skirmishes between fishermen and dam builders over the years, which is something I can relate to as an avid salmon fisherman myself.

The road headed up to Crater Lake (my GPS indicated I had climbed to 7,122 feet above sea level, and the temperature was 20°F cooler up there), which was formed by the volcanic eruption of Mount Mazama. When the magma became depleted, the mountain caved in on itself, forming the crater now hosting the lake. It is the deepest lake in the United States, according to the forest ranger I met who was anxious to educate anyone who would listen. Pretty cool!

I took the mandatory photo and then followed another mountain highway back down towards the Klamath River, which is also rich in history. For the gold buffs, during the latter days of the California Gold Rush, miners would work the streams in the Klamath River region in search of gold.

At the town of Klamath, I turned onto Oregon Route 66 (same name as the other legendary route, but not related) to start heading back to Medford. This beautiful highway passes over the northern edge of the Siskiyou Mountains, with plenty of signs warning "Livestock! Open Range." As I came around a bend, there was a big white bull standing right beside the road. He kindly waited until I passed (luckily) before venturing across. I interpreted this as an omen that the stock market is going to be a good place to invest for the next few years.

Oh, you think I'm just being superstitious? Correct you are, but there is a precedent I should share with you. Years ago, I went to Alaska with a group of fellow fly fishermen. On the last day of our trip, we were trout fishing and I wasn't having any luck with the flies I had with me (and the one guy who had just the *right* streamers was catching fish but not sharing). I got a bit ahead of the group, rounded a bend in the river, and not a hundred feet in front of me was a gigantic Kodiak bear. In a blink, he rushed towards me. (Remember, fellow mavericks, *never panic!*)

I raised my arms and shouted some loud obscenities while standing firm and looking him straight in the eyes (even though I was scared to death). There was no shortage of stories back at the lodge about fishermen who ran away from bears, and none of those stories ended well for the fishermen. He stopped about ten feet in front of me, must have decided I didn't look like food, turned tail, and headed into the bush.

When we were back home, one of the other fishermen (who also worked in the investment industry) jokingly recited the tale to a newspaper columnist friend of ours, who in turn retold it in his column, adding that "It looks like Mal frightened away the bear. We're heading for a bull market!" The long bull run of the '90s began in earnest soon afterwards. So on occasion, superstition is warranted.

If you're planning to do your own stock picking, be prepared to devote more time and effort than it would take if you were just using mutual funds. Researching mutual funds is no walk in the park, but once you have finally selected a fund, it already contains dozens and sometimes hundreds of stocks picked by a pro (overkill, in my opinion). Analyzing each individual stock you will buy (plus those you will decide *not* to buy) is going to require the same effort as studying just one mutual fund.

Many people believe picking a stock is as simple as reading about the company in the press or in a research report, or they pick a stock based on liking what the company does or its product line. This does work in isolated circumstances. When touring the editorial department of a newspaper a long time ago, I was surprised that the layout of the paper was accomplished by pinning typed articles and photos onto bristol boards. I looked into publishing software available at the time—CorelDRAW and Adobe PageMaker, for example—and bought those stocks. I did well for clients.

Actually, it is that simple to pick stocks and invest in

them; you just aren't likely to be making any money doing it in a random fashion.

The stock price of a company represents the sum total of everyone's expectations about the management team's capabilities, the potential for the business, the industry it's in, the outlook for the overall stock and bond markets, and the consensus forecast for the domestic economy and the global economy, all adjusted for risk. If your going to do it as a hobby (refer back to the Introduction), then fine. Build a portfolio of household names and fiddle around with the weight invested in each stock. Perhaps even add a few stocks based on tips from your broker or a technical analyst (they study stock charts to come up with recommendations) to add a little spice. But if you plan to do it seriously, you will have to do some work.

Above, I wrote about my day trip experience in Oregon in order to convey a message. I could have simply written:

- I went on a day trip.
- I took a ride up into the mountains.
- I spent the day visiting some of the local attractions.

Instead, I conducted a bit of research to better understand where I was going and what I might see. I then wrote what I considered to be the more relevant facts associated with the actual ride to convey to you the reasoning for my deciding to take the route I chose. Sort of like a research report.

I made a decision and shared with you my analysis in support of the decision (the route). It's an example of the process you will go through if picking stocks is a passion rather than just a hobby. I do not intend to teach you security analysis. There are as many reference books you can study as there are courses you can take to become a better analyst. The following two paragraphs are quoted from an article I wrote that was published in the July/August 1984 issue of the *Financial Analysts Journal* entitled "The Origin of Fundamental Analysis":

> The fundamental analyst would like to explain potentially different phenomena, but his motives and methods for studying the economy are much the same as the naturalist's contemplating his environment. Macroeconomic constraints analogous to climate and geography in the natural scientist's scheme of things necessarily determine the structures of industries.
>
> A process analogous to natural selection in the animal kingdom is also at work in the world of business, but unlike the natural scientist, however, the fundamental analyst not only seeks to explain the survival of the fittest industries but also to use his restricted understanding to discern which of the many corporate species are fit and which are suited to weather unforeseeable dramatic environmental changes. He endeavors to discover which will be fit.

I admit to using too many big words, probably to compensate for my inexperience back then. When doing your own analysis, think like Charles Darwin and of "survival of the fittest." Use whatever information and tools you can access to determine why a company is doing well in its industry (environment) and whether or not it's fit enough not just to survive but to thrive. Does it have the potential for revenue growth or improvement, enough cash flow to fund its business initiatives, and reasonable finances? If it's lacking financial strength, do you believe that some imminent change in its environment will favour its success in the foreseeable future?

Be careful not to get too carried away with researching your ideas. There are countless studies suggesting that more information does not help you make better decisions. It isn't the analysis that will make you money. Applying a maverick investment philosophy to your decisions, once you have completed enough analysis to support your decision, is what will help you grow your savings.

Myth: All available information is reflected in the stock price.

The stock price reflects everyone's *expectations* (at least of those who are paying attention) but not all *information*.

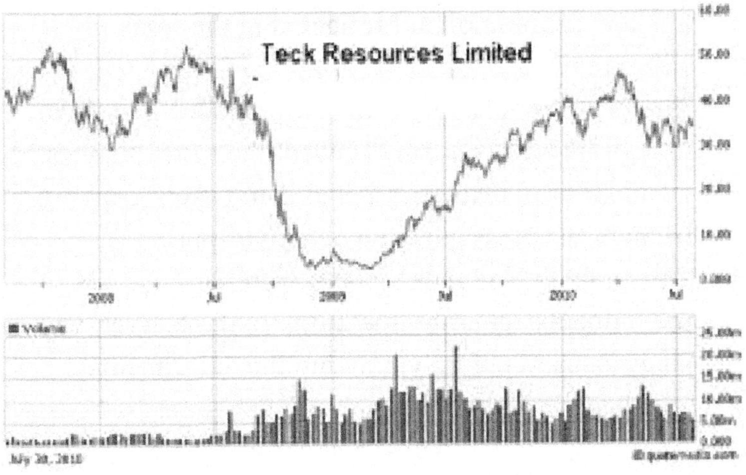

Have a gander at the chart showing the three-year history of the stock price for Teck Resources Limited, a large Canadian mining company focused on copper, metallurgical coal, zinc, and energy. In late 2008 and early 2009, the consensus expectation was that Teck might become bankrupt. The company owed a lot of money (debt) and a global recession was underway. The stock price was undeniably at a low point. Expectations embedded in Teck's depressed stock price were:

- increasing earnings losses
- no recovery in demand for resources—economies were hurting worldwide
- potential insolvency

Putting on your maverick investor cap, you should be asking yourself if this is what is expected, then how much worse can it get? A pessimist can come up with lots of theories on how much worse it can get, but the market has already assigned a price based on such theories coming true. Here is the information not reflected in the stock price:

- The press regularly published evidence that even though China's economy slowed (the world's largest customer for resources), it did not stop growing (though the press gave it a negative spin).
- The real value of Teck's assets were far in excess of the value assigned by the stock market. Even bad analysts were publicly drawing this conclusion.
- Markets always recover.

I am oversimplifying, but even I would get bored listing all of the reasons a maverick would find the stock attractive at the time. In a previous chapter, we hinted that there is a fine line between investing and gambling. When the odds are skewed a great deal in favour of making the bet, it's investing. If there's no rationale for making the bet other than the thrill of perhaps winning, then it's gambling.

In the spring of 2005, I went on a motorcycle tour of Australia with my daughter. On our way back, we had a rather long wait for our connecting flight at Los Angeles International Airport. My daughter was keen to see anything *at all* in California (she was twelve at the time), so we took the bus to Santa Monica. The street mall we visited didn't have many shoppers, but one store was packed to the hilt. We'd never seen an Apple Store in Canada, and the experience was pretty remarkable.

Apple had been the subject of much controversy of late, mostly related to a significant shift in strategy. They began collaborating with Intel, which confused many research analysts and introduced some uncertainty about the potential success of the initiative. Founded in 1968, originally as Integrated Electronics Corporation, Intel is the world's largest semiconductor manufacturer and invented many microprocessors now in the majority of computers. Apple was very protective about its proprietary technology for most of its history and was now suddenly sharing with a huge mass producer supplying microchips to its competitors.

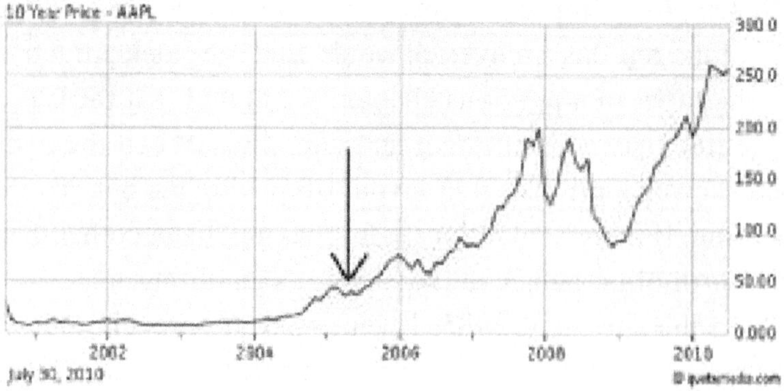

Inspired by the activity in the Apple Store, I did some work on the stock upon my return home. It had traded down some, in sympathy with other tech stocks at the time, and Apple was releasing press releases such as this:

> CUPERTINO, California—March 2, 2005—Apple today announced that music fans have purchased and downloaded more than 300 million songs from the iTunes Music Store. Additionally, the benefit single "Across the Universe," available exclusively on the iTunes Music Store, debuted as number 22 on the Billboard Hot 100 singles chart making it the most successful exclusive digital track ever in its first week of release.

In my opinion, my first upbeat experience in the store and this supporting information (there was more of it if one cared to keep looking) was not truly reflected in the stock price in the spring of 2005.

I could go on and on with similar examples, but the point is a maverick investor will buy stocks for good reasons rather than hearsay or because it's a popular stock to buy. It is important to keep in mind that having a diversified portfolio of stocks all having good reasons to go higher is wise because there's always a good chance you might be wrong about an individual stock.

Good representation in a variety of different industry sectors largely independent of one another will reduce the overall riskiness of your portfolio. In this case, risk is simple: some stocks might not go higher simply because they *just don't* (it happens), or perhaps your analysis was flawed or an unpredictable crisis has thrown a wrench into the equation.

I haven't made it explicit, hoping you might pick up on this central theme. You make the most money when you can identify that expectations are significantly different from reality.

As an illustration, consider someone who suffers from agoraphobia, or has an irrational fear of going outside. This person feels that just by leaving the front door it's quite probable that something terrible is going to happen. Although they may know there is only a remote possibility that something untoward might happen when they leave home, their expectations are vastly different based on experience. Now imagine that everyone in the world but you is agoraphobic. There'd be no traffic, no lineups, and undeveloped real estate would be awfully cheap.

When the investing herd is 100% certain that doomsday is nigh, or that a company in trouble has absolutely no hope, then their expectations are irrational just like the agoraphobic's. Very few occurrences (other than things such as day followed by night) have a 100% of probability of happening before the fact.

Once upon a time, I made a speech to an audience of young aspiring financial analysts, hoping to point them towards the maverick way. Using data from an ancient article published in the *Financial Analysts Journal*, I pointed out a disparity in the expectations of investment analysts. Companies that were expected to have outstanding earnings growth actually underperformed (by a very wide margin) those companies that were expected to continue to report disappointing earnings. You may want to reread that sentence. The study simply determined that optimistic earnings forecasts by research analysts usually turned out to be wrong, and the stock prices went down after it happened. Alternatively, analysts were generally too pessimistic about some companies, and after they were proven wrong, the stocks went up and by a lot.

Opportunities are created when expectations are either too pessimistic or too optimistic. When a company simply keeps on delivering what is expected of it, the news is generally benign (having no significant effect) in terms of its impact on the stock price.

Don't Fall in Love with Your Ideas

It's worth revisiting this. Being reasonably patient is one thing, but being stubborn is something else. If it's becoming clear that your analysis was flawed (new information comes out) or a crisis is imminent, don't hesitate to sell a stock. A stock doesn't know *you* own it. A stock can always be bought back, and the commissions on trades are tiny compared to the ups and downs a stock price will make in less than an hour of stock market action.

I have been known to sell a stock that's been crushed in the market because I just got tired of looking at it in my portfolio. Sometimes an unexpected market correction did the damage. If it happened to be in an industry poised for a recovery and I still believed in my reasons for owning at least one stock in that industry, I'd just pick another one. Then when it went higher, I felt like a genius rather than an idiot. An important thing to remember is there are thousands of different stocks to choose from.

Oh, and forget what you paid for a stock. The market price at any given moment is what it's worth—period! So if the stock is moving higher, even though the market price is significantly lower than your cost, rejoice anyway. Many investors become obsessed with breaking even. A maverick investor knows it's not about breaking even, but gradually and methodically getting ahead. No matter what you paid for that one stock, if it's contributing positively to the growth of the portfolio, then your savings have a chance to grow as big and healthy as the giant redwood tree.

CHAPTER 9

ALTERNATIVE INVESTMENTS: A VERY SHORT CHAPTER

I am unequivocally "old school" and cannot offer much advice when it comes to using options and other derivatives, so-called hedge funds or 60/40 funds, or trading in commodities. Throughout my career, my philosophy has been that if I cannot fully understand the security, then I'm not going to get involved. The vast majority of strategies using these financial instruments fall into two camps:

1) Allow an investor to increase risk by using leverage (borrowed money).
2) Provide a means of reducing risk by hedging.

Sorry, but if someone wants to borrow money to make either an investment (an educated bet) or to simply bet on an event, in either case, I consider it gambling plain and simple. Many hedge funds don't really hedge at all and are actually doing the exact opposite. This is why occasionally a hedge fund goes broke.

I recall when Long-Term Capital Management went broke back in the late '90s. They were a U.S. hedge fund that used trading strategies such as fixed-income arbitrage, statistical arbitrage, and pairs trading, combined with high leverage. The failure of the hedge fund led to a massive bailout by other major banks and investment houses, which was supervised by the Federal Reserve. I have no interest in even learning about "arbitrage" or "pairs trading" or any strategy that involves borrowing or using derivatives. Never mind throwing my hard earned money into these strategies. I am also not interested in explaining them in this book.

Financial products using such techniques are loosely regulated, if at all, and the often "spectacular" results, usually presented over very short periods, can't really be audited (to determine if they're true). I find them too convoluted, and I've been in the business thirty years. When you literally cannot figure out how the results can be as good as they are, then it's *caveat emptor*: buyer beware.

To control risk, mainstream portfolio managers often use options such as puts and calls (which I will not explain in this book either) and funds that clone different market indexes using a variety of derivates—*actual* hedging. This is

fine. With considerable self-training, you can do the same. I find it comforting to be able to see and understand where I am going. I want a clear view of the road ahead.

When I have an obstructed view, I have no idea what to expect. More and increasingly complicated securities and strategies are being invented every day by creative graduates from mathematical and engineering schools who managed to find jobs in the investment industry. The more complex the strategy, the more obstructed is my view of what I can reasonably expect.

CHAPTER 10

WEALTH MANAGEMENT: HUNTING FOR A MAVERICK

If you'd rather leave the job of managing money to professionals, honing your maverick skills will better equip you to find a suitable portfolio manager, whether they work in the wealth management division of a larger financial services company or are employed at or own a boutique wealth management firm.

Larger firms are especially good at marketing their wares, and I would recommend once again that it is better to find the right portfolio manager than to just agree to hire the first one you see. Many portfolio managers aren't good with people, so usually there will be a "client representative" that you will have to contend with first. Insist on meeting with at least one of the people who will actually be making investment decisions on your behalf. Ask questions in the same manner you would if you were interviewing a new investment advisor. For example, ask exactly how they handled themselves in a financial crisis.

The following is an excerpt from a note I sent out to clients. It might serve as a good example of what to look for:

Even though it is extremely difficult (perhaps impossible) to consistently predict market declines, there's plenty of evidence to suggest you can do something about your circumstances once the proverbial poop hits the fan. Fund managers often respond differently depending upon depth of experience or temperament:

- Some are no more experienced (or no smarter) than retail clients—they panic and sell at the bottom of markets.
- Some proclaim a new respect for caution and hold more cash and bonds...after selling at the bottom.
- Some say they're cautious and secretly buy stuff, expecting a rebound (only a "little" dishonest, but this is not a business suited for even "a little" dishonesty).
- Some boldly acknowledge they didn't see the bear coming, apologize, and admit that they are buying cheap assets aggressively "near" the bottom (mavericks).

Asking tough questions will enable you to determine whether you're talking to a fellow maverick or not. Don't be afraid to sound stupid—it's your money we're talking about here and not your ego.

You may want to stay with the big firm you're banking with for convenience or choose to find a smaller firm more specialized in managing money for individuals. It's much easier to learn about what motivates the professionals in a smaller wealth management boutique and discover whether or not their investment style is consistent with your own beliefs, and you will receive a far more customized level of service.

Heads up! When a firm's performance presented to you seems too good to be true, it probably is. A prime example that received considerable attention was the case of Bernie Madoff.

In March 2009, Madoff pleaded guilty to eleven federal crimes and admitted to turning his wealth management business into a massive Ponzi scheme that defrauded thousands of investors out of billions of dollars. Madoff said he began the Ponzi scheme in the early '90s. However, federal investigators believe the fraud began as early as the '80s and that the investment operation may have never been legitimate.

Even small wealth management companies ordinarily have their performance numbers calculated and audited by third-party services. Make sure an independent third party is vetting any performance data you see. Although instances of fraud get volumes of press coverage, they are one in millions. It's sort of like the criminal bikers, or "one percenters" as they're often called. In actuality, the percentage of criminal bikers to ordinary bike enthusiasts is far less than 1%.

Most boutique investment firms aren't gifted marketers, and they rely heavily on word of mouth to get new clients. Ask your friends, accountant, or lawyer for referrals. There's no harm calling and arranging to visit a few firms listed in the phone directory or on the Internet. You will know when you've found the right one—it will feel just like one biker meeting another biker. The following are some useful tips:

- Never hire a wealth management firm based only on past performance.
- Don't complain about investment results; ask for an explanation.
- Never second-guess a portfolio manager.
- Pay the fees—sure they hurt when performance is poor, but you won't care at all when performance is good.
- Be patient; good things don't happen overnight or every day.
- Most important, don't pretend to be smarter than your portfolio manager(s); you're not!

Consider an Investment Buffet

You may want to hire a capable wealth management company to look after the bulk of your savings, while choosing to dabble in mutual funds and/or the stock market with the rest. Provided you stick to your maverick investor principles, you will be successful.

PART FOUR

HOW A MAVERICK INVESTOR MEASURES PROGRESS

CHAPTER 11

ARE YOU ON THE RIGHT TRAIL?

One of modern society's greatest flaws and also its greatest blessing is its obsession with growth. We are taught to covet everything our neighbours have and then some. Winning is everything.

Why is this flawed? There are always natural limits to growth. If you manage to acquire everything your neighbours have to the point where they have nothing and you have it all, it's inevitable that things will get nasty and some event will tip the balance back in their favour...perhaps a gunshot.

However, this obsession has also contributed to the incredible progress in technology, comfortable living circumstances for more and more people, and global wealth. Wanting more *drives* progress, and progress gives us the generous fruits of a capitalist society.

You have a new car, a nice house, and toys, and all these are evidence that you are personally making progress. But how do you determine you are making progress with your investment portfolio? Just like how your own journey through life suffers from occasional bumps in the road, you should expect no less from your investments.

Have a look at the following chart:

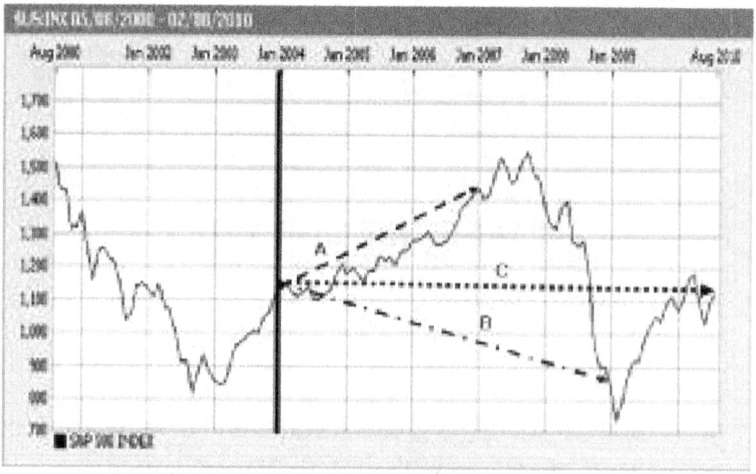

A: January 2004 to Jan 2007 = Happy (positive slope means + returns)
B: January 2004 to Jan 2009 = Miserable (negative slope – losses)
C: January 2004 to August 2010 = Confused (no progress)

Measuring progress isn't easy. Do you judge your personal worth higher when you have a thriving career and many material things? Did your assessment of self-worth drop during the brief time you were unemployed and in debt up to your ears? I suppose the correct answer depends upon your own sense of values, but, in general, self-esteem will change with your circumstances to some extent.

Investment performance is particularly biased by when you choose to measure it. The graph is just the value of the S&P 500 over the past ten years. Assuming an investor simply bought a fund that mirrored the index around January 1, 2004, we can see how important it is when we judge progress:

1) If an investor called their advisor up on January 1, 2007, they would have been pleased to discover the investment

was worth much more over just three years. The upward slope of the line shows that the rate of return was nicely positive (it's just math).

2) Just two years later, things have changed dramatically. The downward slope would suggest a very negative rate of return. No doubt, a rather unpleasant chat with the advisor would follow.
3) The investor might notice that more recently the total value of their savings has rebounded strongly in the short term but overall can't help but feel disappointed since the value of the portfolio is still marginally less than it was when first invested in January 2004.

Judging by the lack of progress made at point 3, it would seem buy and hold definitely isn't the bee's knees that it's made out to be.

Timing Is Everything

Don't be fooled. Over the years, there have been many endpoints that, depending on your starting point, would have made even a buy-and-hold strategy look okay. Timing is everything. It should also be clear that if you managed to get out of the stock market on some of those higher notes (doesn't have to be the peaks) and reinvested on lower notes (doesn't have to be the trough either), the results would be much better overall.

The vast majority of investors make their first foray into the markets at the worst possible time. Don't be embarrassed by it, since it has everything to do with our species' ingrained propensity to follow the herd. If you, like most people, suffered after buying at a market top, start buying and selling more deliberately at times you deem to be more intelligent. Developing a maverick mindset will easily correct the first error in timing if applied over time.

A maverick investor isn't obsessed with growth. Unadulterated greed is not motivating to the maverick, but rather growth is the journey and making progress is the objective. Understanding the arithmetic of performance and its biases is much akin to knowing there will be ups and downs, detours, and occasional roadblocks, and following the best trail possible despite these challenges will be fun and progressive.

Don't Blame the Guide

Unless your advisor knows you and you know your advisor very well, it's pretty difficult to communicate efficiently. If they disagree with what you want to do, or vice versa, chances are you will win. After all, they don't want to lose your business. The deck is stacked in your favour, so when the crap hits the fan (a market crisis or just a bad stock pick), it is futile to assign blame.

A friend of mine who is the CEO of a U.S. mutual fund company headquartered in San Antonio, Texas, taught me a valuable lesson in people management. Most disagreeable things that happen are caused by events outside of our direct control—they come from the outside world. In maverick fashion, he made it clear to his entire staff that under no circumstances would finger-pointing (assigning blame) be tolerated. Everyone's immediate goal was to collectively work towards solving the problem and should never even attempt to lay blame on another person or they'd get the social equivalent of a pistol-whipping (it is Texas after all). The result was an organizational culture that is happy and efficient.

When it comes to communicating with or passing judgement on your advisor's contribution to your investment program, it's best to avoid trying to determine whether it was you or the advisor who screwed up. Neither of you are to blame, but together you are the solution.

It doesn't matter what price was originally paid for individual stocks, or what the unit value was when you purchased a mutual fund, or what the total portfolio value was when you first hired your wealth manager. Based on the timing of your first foray into markets and what has transpired since then to the current endpoint, if you are satisfied that progress has been made, then stay with the program. Having more money invested than when you started or gaining back some ground if your starting point was bad are good signs. Both you and your advisor will get better at maverick investing with experience.

As teenagers, we believed we knew everything, but as we get older, we are constantly humbled by what little we actually do know. This isn't much different from maturing as an investor. We come to know some things extremely well, such as what temptations to avoid and how human behaviour in some situations is quite predictable. These few things we do know are but a microscopic speck of dust compared to the world of things we don't. The maverick investor at least tries to use what little they know to make better investment decisions.

CHAPTER 12

THE ECONOMY, OR THE REALLY BIG PICTURE

There's a saying that goes, "It helps to know where you've been to know where to go." I think we should add, "It helps to know where you are!"

When it comes to investments, timing has everything to do with the business cycle. The picture below is a bit cluttered, but the text in white identifies what stage the stock market should be at (always one step ahead of the economy) compared to where the economy would be during the typical stages of an the economic cycle:

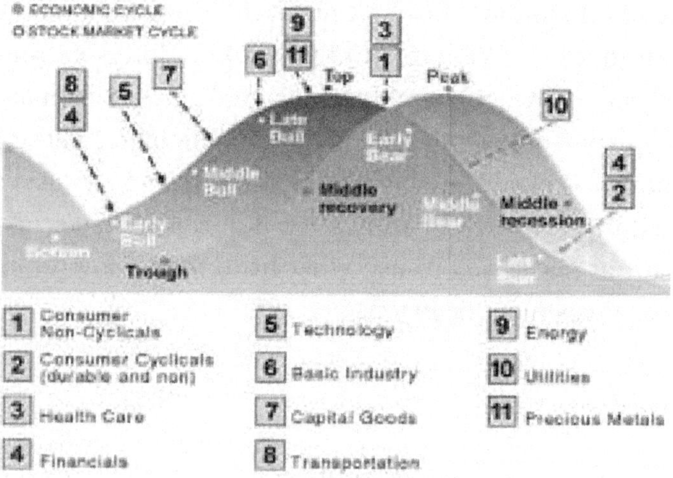

The stock market will begin rising even before the economy has reached its bottom. I've mentioned a few signals in previous chapters that will get an investment maverick's senses tingling. When the general mood of investors as reflected in the press or analyst reports is doom and gloom, but the stock market seems to be going up, then change for the better is afoot. If at the same time reasonably good statistics are coming out but are interpreted in a glass-half-empty sort of way, this is also supportive that it might just be a good time to be invested in stocks. Of course, if the economy is still trying to find its legs, the bad news stories will still outnumber the good news stories. Below is an example of a news item:

> The Chicago PMI unexpectedly rose for the first time since April. The diffusion index climbed to 62.3 in July from 59.1 in June, the highest since February. By this measure alone, activity should be (again...should be) picking up in coming months. New orders gained 5 points to 64.6, employment rose a couple of points to 56.6, production gained a point to 65.0, the order backlog jumped nearly 7 points to 57.6, and inventories started to expand again. Even the prices component slipped. All in, a good report in contrast to a couple of the other regional surveys (Empire, Philly).

If reports like these were coming out when the stock market was reaching all time highs, a maverick investor would ignore them. [You don't really have to fully understand the Purchasing Managers Index (PMI) but can learn a bit about it quickly on the Internet.] *Good* news is *not news* in a bull market. However, if the stock market has barely recovered from some recent crisis or recently suffered a correction, then the news bodes well. If you add to this that companies are generally reporting earnings better than analysts were expecting and other similar encouraging news items, then we start to see a more optimistic picture developing while the rest of the investment herd wallows in misery.

Different sectors do perform better or worse at different times during a cycle. Some investors try to "sector rotate" based on the general pattern, but every cycle is unique and has its stars and dogs. By now you should be wary of adopting any pattern that is "expected" since it's the unexpected that makes more money. Think of the business cycle as night and day: it's certain that we will have cycle lows and highs. The difference is there's no predicting with precision when the lows and highs will happen. And isn't it what you do during your days and nights that matter most? Day will follow night, but it's what you do to prepare for your days and your nights that make life interesting and rewarding.

I certainly can't be bothered examining every type of indicator that I've used or others use to help them make "big picture" investment decisions. One that is worthy of learning more about is interest rates. Ever since the Nobel Prize–winning economist and statistician Milton Friedman began modelling money supply and its impact on the economy, world leaders have attempted to influence the business cycle using interest rates as their weapon of choice.

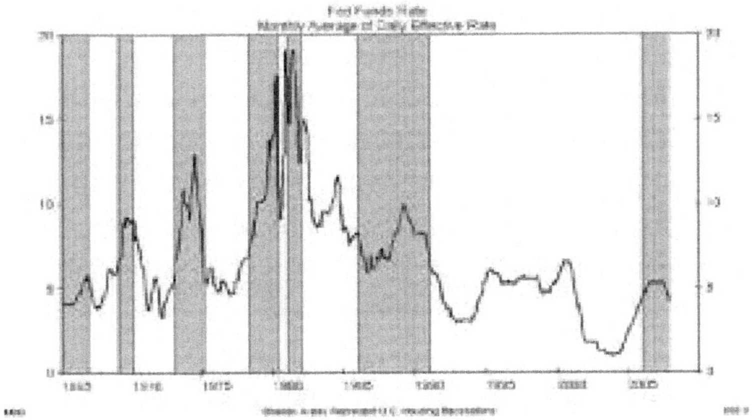

It isn't the actual interest rate that matters so much, but rather the direction rates are going—up or down. The graph shows U.S. housing market recessions (shaded areas) and the trend in interest rates (the line). When rates are rising, there's almost always a housing recession at the same time.

The government *raises* the level of interest rates to slow down an overheated economy where the threat of uncontrollable price inflation becomes a real possibility. The central bank, on the other hand, will *lower* interest rates once they feel that the slowdown in economic activity, or even a recession, has tempered inflation expectations. They will try to reignite consumer spending and encourage businesses to invest capital and start growing (stop downsizing) again. When interest rates get to zero, the economy is usually in such dire straights that deflation is a worry. Deflation (a falling general level of prices) is associated with economic depressions, and nobody wants that.

Investors are wise to exit the stock market when the headlines and other signals discussed in earlier chapters suggest that market sentiment is at the point of maximum bliss. It's not unusual to miss the peak and hang in there just a bit too long, so if you notice interest rates are trending higher, which will certainly cause a market correction, then it's time to sell stocks and move into short-term securities or value stocks. In fact, interest rates for bonds will begin rising even before the government starts trying to influence them using its own tools. This is because bond portfolio managers have consulted their crystal balls and are already bracing for government intervention.

Interest rates will stop rising at some point during the economic slump. At this point, the mood reflected in the press and financial community in general will be extremely gloomy. It will be wise to buy into bonds or bond funds. As interest rates decline during the tail end of the recession, bond prices will rise (it's just math, accept it). It's also a good time to begin moving into high-growth stocks (or smaller companies), which tend to rise aggressively from very low recessionary levels in a falling interest rate environment.

You need to know where you are
before you can know where to go.

Once you have a sense of where you are in a cycle, it's much easier to figure out where you should be going. From that vantage point, you are able to have a look around and determine the most promising path. Industries go through boom and bust periods, just like we do. By staying reasonably informed about conditions in the current business world (housing, automobiles, technology, pharmaceuticals, retailing, and so on), you will be the best judge of which firms and industries are poised to perform the best in the next stage of an economic cycle. It's far more rewarding to pinpoint stocks that *will* do well (unexpectedly) than it is to sit on the shares of companies everyone agrees *are* doing well.

By definition, all cycles go round and round. But like the shiny new wheels and tires now on my Harley, although they still just go round and round, they *are* new and *look* different.

I don't ordinarily ride at night. It's kind of like investing using only stock quotes but no news services. But once my new tires and wheels arrived late in the afternoon, I wanted to at least get from Medford to the Portland area to spend the night. I arrived at my hotel very late and woke up very early to begin my journey back eastward. It was a cool 60°F (16°C) morning in Portland.

The historical route running along the Columbia River, the Oregon Trail, was first trail-blazed by the expedition team headed by the U.S. army soldiers Meriwether Lewis and William Clark, with the assistance of Sacajawea and her husband, Toussaint Charbonneau. And what a trail they did blaze. The Columbia River Gorge is an eyeful to behold, and no wonder it's considered a national treasure. I wonder what the expedition team would say today if they could see the countless trains headed both east and west along their trail. Like the St. Lawrence River for Canadians in the east, the mighty Columbia River became an artery for commerce and development in the Pacific Northwest.

The ride from Oregon (60°F/16°C in the morning) to Idaho (100°F/38°C through what is often called the Oregon High Desert) was no cakewalk, but it was interesting. From cherry and tree farming (now I know where some of those more mature poplar trees the major cities buy to line streets actually come from) to relatively barren and arid mountain passes, the ride was both challenging and a scenic kaleidoscope. It was evident that the further east I travelled, the hotter and more arid the countryside became.

The High Desert returned to some semblance of life as I approached Boise, Idaho. Irrigated potato fields intermingled with cattle ranches provided a more relaxed scenic prelude before riding into Boise proper, the capital and largest city of the State of Idaho. It's barely the hundredth largest city in America (a population of over 500,000), but it is clearly the business and banking centre of Idaho.

Are There Stocks for All Seasons?

Besides cyclicality, seasonality does play a part in market behaviour. The market typically (though not always) flounders a touch in January and February after the holiday season. There are many theories, but, once again, the easiest way to interpret market behaviour is by thinking about the behaviour of people who make up the market. There's always the winter vacation, and the shopping frenzy during late December and early January of every year puts quite a dent in everyone's budget.

By March and April, markets ordinarily are healthier (going up). There is a proliferation of marketing initiatives from mutual fund companies and financial services firms to encourage saving for retirement, and those reckless shoppers are susceptible to any pitch hinting they might be able to invest and recover some of the money they've blown.

There's an adage "sell in May and go away" that for the most part is pretty accurate. In my experience, it's perfectly fine to delay any portfolio shifts until mid- to late June. If you feel like exploiting trends like these, the choice between moving some funds out of stocks and into either bonds or short-term securities depends on where you are in the economic or business cycle. You should be able to figure out what I mean by now.

Although the resources sector and basic industries (steel, manufacturing, etc.) and even retailing businesses are particularly vulnerable to the "summer doldrums," others can actually perform very well in the summer. Below is a stock chart of Agrium Inc., a Canadian company that produces and sells fertilizers and agricultural supplies in North America and the rest of the world.

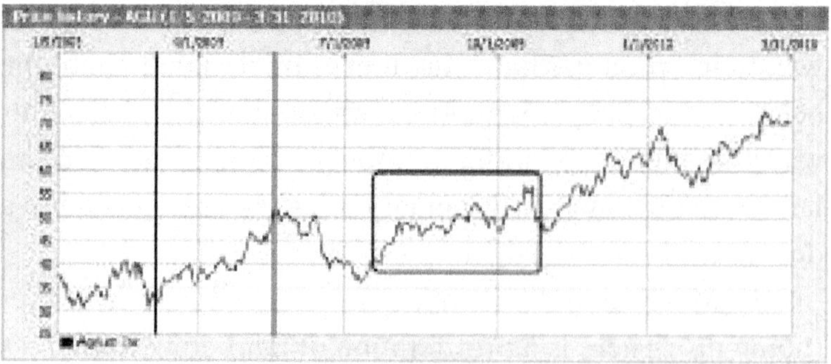

I used the one-year 2009 price behaviour for Agrium in the chart, but the pattern is consistent most years.

Between mid-February and June, this stock will do okay mostly because the market is generally doing better. However, if there are issues specific to the agricultural industry, it may lag the market. For example, natural gas is an important cost in nitrogen-based fertilizer production, so if gas prices are very high, profits may suffer. Are you getting a feel for how the various and complex economic and industry factors influence matters?

If there are no unusual issues for the company and industry to contend with, then the stock will also suffer from the "sell in May and go away" phenomenon just like the overall stock market. What is unique to the industry, however, is that planting season is well underway by July and related news concerning crop production and commodity pricing draws attention to the industry during the mid-summer months.

In the simplest terms, if there's a decent growing season and reasonable pricing for corn, wheat, and the larger foodstuffs, then the demand for fertilizer for the following year should be very strong. The market is always one step ahead, so if the agricultural industry's future revenues and profits are expected to be better (fertilizers, farm equipment manufacturers, and such), then the stocks move higher despite the lethargy of the overall stock market during the summer.

You may have noticed that retailing stocks (department stores and specialty chains) begin moving higher in the fall months in anticipation of the shopping season. An important consideration these days is determining what items shoppers seek as gifts. Manufacturers and distributors of mobile phones, computers and accessories, and even video games are now more sensitive to the same seasonality that used to be (years ago) confined to just retailing companies and toy manufacturers.

The overall stock market does well from about mid-August until September when investors are back from summer holidays and are again focusing on trying to make some money rather than spend it. Resources and basic industries usually rebound the most, having been neglected the most, but industries sensitive to consumer spending (such as computers, telecommunications, and retailing) in the latter months of the year also see some positive price momentum. September and October are almost always terrible. I've never understood it but have learned the hard way that there is no point pretending it isn't going to happen. It's best to just wait it out, or maybe buy a little more of your favourite stocks or funds during weakness, because November and December usually witness strong rebounds in stock markets to end a typical year. When the market ends the year on its high note, you should remove the extra money you added to your investments during September/October.

CHAPTER 13

FIGURING OUT WHERE YOU ARE, OR "YOU ARE HERE"

Downtown Boise, Idaho, is quite a nice place to spend an evening. There are plenty of quaint restaurants and some nice jazz clubs all within a couple of short blocks' walking distance, and the area includes a vibrant section known as the Basque Block. Boise's Basque community is the second largest such community in the United States.

Early the next morning, I pulled out my map and marked, "You are here!" I decided to visit a relative who lived on the border of Idaho and Wyoming in the village of Victor, Idaho, and headed east. You really can tell when you are getting closer to Wyoming and the Teton Range. Cement factories seem less prevalent (there must be lots of lime deposits in Idaho) and suddenly everything is green. The ride to Victor, nestled in the lovely Teton Valley was a joy. An even greater joy for me was that it was open mic night at the local watering hole.

I was reluctant to ask to borrow a guitar or sit at the drums, since these local boys brought their own gear so *they* could play them. Instead, I let them do the hard work while I just sang “Roadhouse Blues” (an appropriate tune for the venue, I thought). Of course, with a few bolts of Jack Daniels under your belt, it’s easy to believe you’re Jim Morrison for a few minutes. I hoped the other patrons had imbibed with as much gusto as I had and that their hearing became just as distorted.

The following morning, I was off through the beautiful Teton Pass into Wyoming. The Grand Teton mountain range and Wyoming’s Grand Teton National Park are as scenic in the summer as in the winter. (Also, since *Grand Teton* in French translates to “large tit,” and we Canadians know a bit of French, I found myself chuckling at the name—though the official claim is that it was named after the Teton Sioux.) Having skied the area many moons ago, I still remember the pristine white snowfalls in these mountains, the amazing hot springs, and trout streams running into the Snake River basin. Seeing a small herd of bison grazing with the mountains as a backdrop in summer is easily as soothing a sight to behold.

The ride from Jackson Hole through Dubois, the authentic western town located along the Wind River was nothing short of majestic. The Absaroka and Wind River Ranges play havoc with your visual sense, and it seems you've landed on another planet after every curve in the road.

The striking realization that human ingenuity managed to surmount all of these geological barriers, and in many cases convert such obstacles into some variety of recreation, is quite humbling. Of course, on occasion, human ingenuity is a pain in the butt. One road through the Rockies was under construction for a seventeen-mile stretch. Down to one lane of dirt and gravel, the waiting in lines of vehicles alternating just to get through, is frustrating enough in a temperature-regulated automobile. On a motorcycle, it's a dusty and exhausting experience. You don't have to be a physicist to know that an 850-pound vehicle on two wheels is not stable on dirt and loose gravel. If one wheel slips, down goes the bike (and rider too).

Due to the roadwork delay and slower speeds along mountain roads with tight curves, it took me ten hours to get to Sturgis for the first day of the infamous Sturgis Motorcycle Rally. All night and day, the sweet sound of rumbling Harley-Davidson engines could be heard in and around the city jam-packed with bikers.

You Are Here!

After many years in the investment business, the most common grief I hear from individual investors is not being able to identify where we are in a given cycle. Seasons are predictable enough but not of much value if there is a crisis of some sort lurking to eat away all the good performance you've worked hard to earn.

Many portfolio managers and some strategists (aka experts) insist that you can't time markets, so why bother trying? I've already explained why financial services firms would prefer you didn't try to adjust your portfolio, so at the very least some of their advice on this front must be taken with a grain of salt. I agree that you cannot *predict* the anomalous changes in market psychology that influence both the economy and the general direction of stock prices. However, it's not *predicting* that will either salvage your savings or grow them; rather, it's the maverick practice of *anticipating* behaviour and acting upon it in a rational way that will help.

I am loath to get into the quantitative measures I use, because they are useful for me and the numbers aren't remotely as important as the interpretation of them (a constant theme throughout this guidebook). Having figured out *where you are* at any point along your journey, any strategic planning you do is only meaningful from that starting point. Once things change (i.e. you move along or your environment changes), so will your conclusions.

I will demonstrate using a couple of common investment tools that I consider relevant today. The time of this writing is early August 2010. Whenever referring to the following thoughts, remember that everything you read may already be obsolete by the time you read it.

I've already mentioned some relatively current (i.e. July 2010) trends catching my attention. The more important one is the market slowly drifting higher from the summer doldrums (seasonality) as companies continue to report "better than expected" earnings. With market sentiment still quite pessimistic, I'd like to confirm my suspicions that the maverick investor should instead be optimistic. You now know that this difference is what makes for opportunities.

Many screening devices are free on the Internet or are available through your online service provider. These tools are often used to isolate stocks with attractive characteristics. I will use them occasionally to try to discern what sorts of stocks are moving (up or down) or leading the market higher. At the time of writing, I discovered that the stronger stocks exhibited the following features:

- price momentum
- sales momentum
- earnings momentum

You can probably guess that price momentum is a bit of double counting, since if I screen for stocks with rising prices, they should have price momentum—this is a bit circular. But sales momentum and rising earnings are not always drivers of price momentum. We talked about how supply and demand for a stock drives its price, not earnings or sales growth per se.

While the investing herd is heavily into bonds and short-term securities (safety and value bias), growth stocks are where they *will* want to be soon. A maverick investor is justified in *anticipating* rising demand for stocks with these attributes. As discussed briefly at the beginning of Chapter 12, this is typically what happens in the early to mid stages of a bull market cycle. Technology stocks (high beta) are strong, but not surprisingly, we're seeing market leadership right *now* in agricultural machinery (seasonal), auto parts, and aluminum and coal (basic industries). Weaker performing sectors *now* include home appliances (seasonal), drug stores, and medical services (normally defensive or value stocks that held up better during the early summer but aren't moving now).

The prevailing mood in the press is *anxiety* and forecasts call for continuing struggles for the automotive industry and a weak economy for the next several months. All of this information is music to a maverick investor's ears, since (smart money) buying behaviour reflects the opposite. The sectors moving (being bought or accumulated) tell me the economy is improving.

Rather than nitpick through data, which is seldom interesting reading, I'll highlight three graphs to relate where I think we are today. You can find charts like this easily online, but these are courtesy of a strategist friend of mine who is one of the good ones.

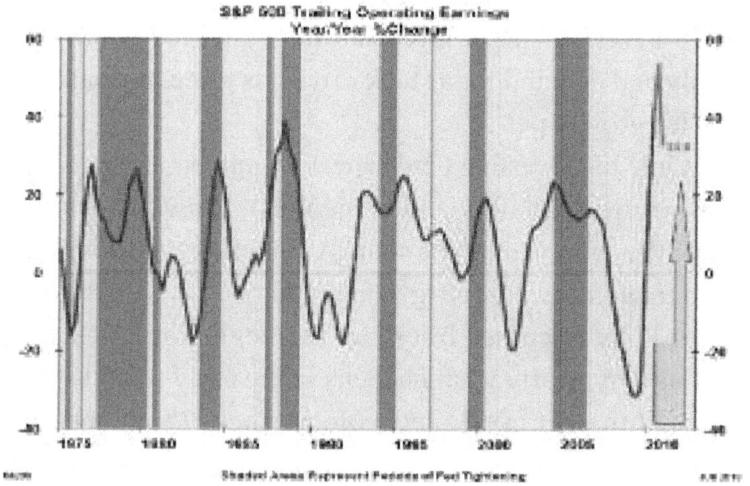

The earnings recovery underway now is very robust (see graph above with trailing earnings for the S&P 500—"trailing earnings" are just the last four quarterly earnings reports added together to equal a one-year period to the present). And we already know the rebound was largely unexpected. By the way, the final tip of the line dropping down a notch is this strategist's forecast (to 32.5% year-over-year growth in trailing earnings). Expectations die hard.

Take a look at the graph of the price/earnings (P/E) ratio below for the overall U.S. market. This measure is common, and as I hinted earlier, you can study up on it if you like. Intuitively, it's the price you and I as investors are willing to pay (average of all current stock prices in the index) for a dollar of earnings power companies (on average) in the index will be providing shareholders.

The decline in the P/E ratio can happen because stock prices fall or because earnings rise, or a combination of both. In my view, the best of all scenarios is evident at the time of writing this. Prices fell due to seasonality, but skepticism about corporate profitability also had a negative influence. Glowing earnings reports coming from unexpected industry groups is also making valuations (P/E ratio is considered to be a valuation measure) more attractive since it seems investors are getting surprisingly more earnings power for the price. Lower prices mean better deals.

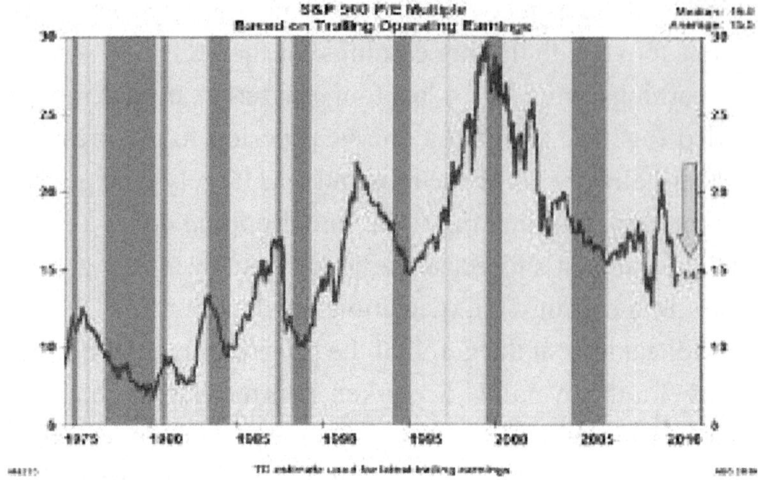

Judging by the rapid recovery in stock prices from their low point last year and the softness of the market more recently, my guess would be we're not at the very earliest stage of a typical cycle, but the economy is still gathering steam after a brief correction.

Consumers are saving more and paying off personal debt (other items worth tracking) and therefore consumer spending is not yet having much of a positive impact on the economy. So what is driving the earnings recovery? The low interest rate policy and government stimulus is encouraging businesses to spend. Businesses invest in capital goods or services to improve productivity. They fired people to cut costs, and before hiring them back, companies upgrade communications networks, manufacturing equipment, and other things that improve productivity without bumping payroll.

Capital spending is ordinarily associated with the mid part of an economic cycle. Don't forget, this example is only good at this one point in time. In early August 2010, there are no indications from the press or most research reports I've read (and I read a lot of them) that investors are aware there is a business cycle ramping up. Based on this short analysis, a maverick investor should be assuming that once the herd figures this all out in the coming months—and the investment herd is notoriously thickheaded, so it might take some time—they will be headed for stocks sensitive to business spending. A maverick investor would want to get there ahead of them.

Coincidence?

You may have caught on to this already. Wouldn't the companies that are enjoying better-than-expected earnings and price momentum be the ones that investors will be attracted to soon and will begin scrambling to buy? Your maverick senses must be tingling.

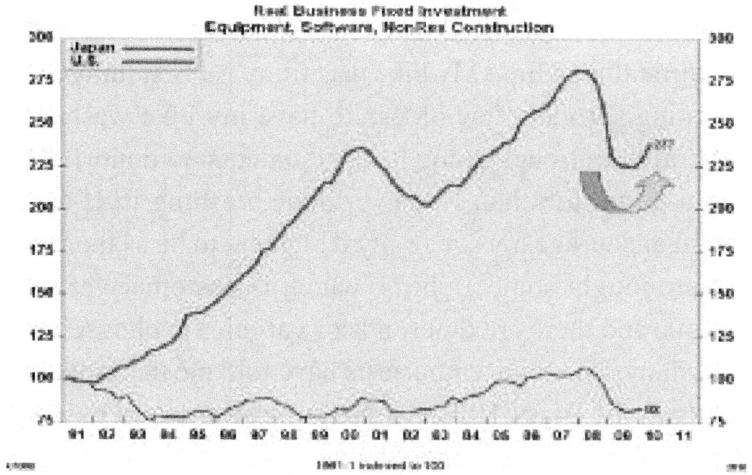

This analysis (in early August 2010 and at no other time) suggests you are here:

- Seasonal low in the market
- In early to mid stage of cycle
- Interest rates remain low, with no threat of inflation
- No imminent threat of an overheated market

This is one of the world's most notorious biker gatherings, in the city of Sturgis near the Black Hills and Badlands of South Dakota. Nearby is Mount Rushmore, which features 60-foot sculptures of the heads of former U.S. presidents Washington, Jefferson, Roosevelt, and Lincoln. Not far away is also Devils Tower, which is the first U.S. National Monument, declared so by President Theodore Roosevelt in 1906.

First things first: My bike was filthy, so first thing in the morning, I rode a few blocks to have my bike washed by several bikini-clad young ladies (students no doubt). They did a better job than I've ever done washing it. If only I could encourage my son or my daughters to be as thorough. I then bought some T-shirts, which is customary at these events, and there are thousands of varieties to choose from.

Many other bike enthusiasts have told me that riding the roads in the Black Hills is a great experience, so I asked a local for suggestions on a day trip and headed out early in the morning. The area is famous for its mining heritage; I rode by the Homestake Mine, which was the largest and deepest gold mine in North America until it shut down in 2002. By then, it had produced $1 billion worth of gold. It's located near Lead, South Dakota. My next stop was

Keystone, where they run tours at the Big Thunder Gold Mine, which was first discovered in 1882. I was more interested in having breakfast in the historic town, having visited my share of mines in Africa, South America, and up in the north as far as the Arctic Ocean.

I vowed not to bother visiting the tourist spots near here, but Keystone is a stone's throw from Mount Rushmore. The presidents whose likenesses are carved into the rock were selected to represent 150 years of American history.

After snapping a photo, I followed the 16A scenic roadway through Black Hills National Forest, and it certainly was an experience. I've never been on a road that switched back over itself (bridges) so often, and riding through the narrow tunnels cut through the hills was just a hoot.

The only downside is that during the rally, there are lots of bikers, and they're all riding the same roads. Once again, traffic ruins the experience. After getting stuck in a line of

Harleys crawling behind a tour bus, I took the first turn I could find and headed back towards Sturgis.

I spent the next couple of days buying stuff for the bike. Did I mention I'm impulsive at times? Vendors from everywhere come to these events, and it is possible to get all kinds of things done: airbrush painting, wheels and tires, and custom parts installed on the spot. Many of these items we don't even see in Canada or would take weeks to have delivered and installed.

Every night there are world-class bands performing all around Sturgis. Some good friends from *American Iron Magazine* picked me up in a rental car. Some drinking might be involved, and our designated driver, the editor of the magazine, prefers sobriety of late. We headed to the legendary Buffalo Chip Campground outside of town, where Bob Dylan would be performing. Tents and campers dot the landscape for what seems like miles around, and bikers wearing a wide variety of costumes pack the huge open-air concert venue. It seems less dress is best for many of the female bikers.

You might be asking yourself, "Isn't it unmaverick-like to attend a huge gathering such as a motorcycle rally?" Crowds are indeed uncomfortable for the independently spirited types. Most of the folks would much rather be out on the open road, and indeed they usually spent a good portion of their day exploring the surrounding terrain on their motorcycles.

I remember when I attended Harley-Davidson's 95th anniversary rally in Milwaukee. During the opening ceremonies, Jay Leno remarked, "There are hundreds of thousands of Harleys here, and no two of them are identical."

I believe these rallies provide a unique setting for thousands of like-minded and independently spirited people to pay homage to freedom. They share a common passion for riding the open road on two-wheeled (and sometimes three-wheeled) machines in the open air, and being able to taste and smell the countryside every inch of the way. It's a rare opportunity to meet one another, share stories, and admire how creatively they've each transformed a factory-built motorcycle or a complete custom chopper into an extension of their own persona.

Before leaving Sturgis, I felt obliged to attend the 2009 AMD World Championship of Custom Bike Building. The proprietor of the shop in Oregon that installed my new wheels for me had entered a custom bike he built from scratch into this competition. He told me he would be ecstatic if he managed to get into the top ten.

I watched his expression go from hopeful to somewhat disappointed as they announced the tenth-, ninth-, and eighth-place winners in reverse sequence. When the announcer proclaimed, "...and from Medford, Oregon..." his demeanour quickly reflected disbelief mingled with joy. His creation won him second place, and the competition was fierce. When Willie G. Davidson, senior vice president and chief styling officer of Harley-Davidson Motor Company, shows up to admire the contestants' entries, you know they're impressive.

PART FIVE

MAVERICK ROAD STORIES

CHAPTER 14

OBSTACLES AND ROADBLOCKS, OR DEALING WITH DISASTER

A few years ago, I was riding with a group of friends through the lovely hills around San Antonio, Texas. It was raining off and on, so the roads were wet and slick. In southern climes, a bit of rain causes the oil on the road surface to become treacherous for motorcycles.

I was leading the pack and signalled that I wanted to pull over into a driveway. I just needed to consult my map. The biker immediately behind me applied his break to slow down, and the invisible oil slick took him and the bike down. Fortunately, he wasn't hurt, but the rental bike had a modest number of damaged parts and scrapes.

The bike could still be ridden, and our friend suggested he would just pay the deductible (which was a lot of money) when returning the bike. Having spent small fortunes on parts and accessories for our own bikes, most of us could tell there was perhaps $500 of damage, and a deductible four times that number wasn't worth paying.

The group decided to make a sport of it. From experience, we knew there was no chance that one dealer would have *all* the parts in stock, so we spent several hours calling to locate the necessary parts and then travelling from one dealer to another having them installed. The morning weather was crappy, but since we had a mission to fulfill, the day was fun and when we were done, the bike was as good as new. The weather improved gradually and later that afternoon, we managed to tour around the area and check out some cool towns and scenic roads on the way to Austin, Texas.

A maverick investor is always prepared to meet calamity head on, recalibrate, and move along. When an investment goes bad, one's first inclination is to go on a rampage and assign blame. It is not unusual for disgruntled investors to join or instigate a class action suit, write letters to the editors of newspapers, and otherwise take aim at company management or their advisors for "getting them into this mess."

I am certain that my friend who dropped his bike, after recovering from the immediate shock, had to control his immediate impulse to attack me for threatening to cut him off. My action of signalling certainly suggested I was about to turn into his path. A maverick himself, he no doubt realized quickly that blaming me would be a futile exercise and decided instead to look himself over for wounds and, after finding nothing serious, get on with repairing the bike.

In my opinion, despite efforts to try to disguise the fact, any event that destroys property or harms a person—either yourself or another—causes grief. When an investment causes one to lose money, it is tantamount to a destruction of extremely personal property. Following the initial shock and disbelief that it could happen at all, overwhelming sadness sets in.

The Kubler-Ross Seven Stages of Grief:

1. Shock and denial
2. Pain and guilt
3. Anger and bargaining
4. Depression, reflection, loneliness
5. The upward turn
6. Reconstruction and working through
7. Acceptance and hope

The more serious the episode causing grief, whether it's a death in the family or losing a job, the longer it takes to get through these stages. Experts assert it is necessary and healthy to work one's way through all stages to recover properly from a grievous event. It is perfectly natural to *feel* your way through the healing process, but when an investor loses money, it is foolhardy to let grief influence decision-making. It's imperative in terms of your actions to skip stages two through five and get on with reconstruction.

I can't count how many investments I've had go sour over thirty years, never mind remember them all. One in particular was a bit unusual, so I do recall some of the details.

In 1997, there was a flurry of stocks issued in Canada using a method concocted by creative investment bankers. They called them "installment receipts." You bought a share of a company but only had to pay *half* the price up front. A year later, you were expected to pay the other half of the price for the share. These installment receipts traded on the stock market too. They sound great, don't they? It's a lot like buying furniture—pay half now and half later.

I had invested client funds in one such issue. The

company was Boliden Limited. Soon after the installment receipts were acquired, the mining company suffered a public relations nightmare. A tailings dam at one of their mines failed on April 25, 1998, and toxic goop flowed out, destroying crops and threatening environmental damage to a national park in Spain. An excerpt from a press release issued about a month later said the following:

> TORONTO, May 27 /CNW-PRN/ – Boliden Limited announced today that The Toronto Stock Exchange (TSE) had suspended trading in Boliden installment receipts (which trade under the symbol BOL.IR). Boliden common shares (which trade under the symbol BOL) continue to trade on the TSE. The installment receipts continue to be traded on the "over-the-counter" market.

The folks who came up with the idea for installment receipts didn't foresee the possibility that the underlying stock could fall so much that the installment receipt itself could have a negative price.

Confused? Say you buy a house for $300,000 and pay only half the price in cash. You mortgage the other half ($150,000). If the market value of the house declines to only $100,000 (which happened to many U.S. homeowners in recent times), then there's a dilemma: the homeowner owes the bank $150,000, but the value of the house (the collateral for the mortgage loan) is only worth $100,000. If the bank forecloses, it loses $50,000. If the homeowner just walks away, at least they're not stuck with paying the bank more than the house is worth.

Investors in the Boliden installment receipts, including myself, were confronted with the same problem. Here is some more of the press release:

> In June and July 1997, Trelleborg International BV, an indirect wholly owned subsidiary of Trelleborg AB, sold 55,898,216 Boliden common shares in a public offering at a price of $16.00 per share payable in two installments. The first installment of $8.00 per share was paid at closing and the second and final installment of $8.00 is payable on or before June 17, 1998. At the closing of the public offering, the Boliden common shares sold by Trelleborg were pledged back to Trelleborg to secure payment of the final installment. Until full payment of the final installment, beneficial ownership of pledged Boliden common shares is represented by the installment receipts.
>
> The TSE stated that it had suspended trading in the installment receipts because the market price of Boliden common shares had fallen below $8.00, the amount of the final installment. As a consequence, in the opinion of the TSE, the installment receipts had, in effect, a negative value. The TSE noted, however, that the suspension from trading is not a reflection or comment on the financial condition of Boliden.

The installment receipt had a negative value, just like the house in my example. The value of the house ($100,000) minus the value of the mortgage ($150,000) means the house is worth -$50,000. Yet investors in the receipts were still obligated to pay the other half of the installment for the stock they bought in Boliden (sort of like the mortgage). The only other option besides refusing to make the second installment was to actually *pay* someone else (a buyer) to take the installment off your (the seller's) hands. This was happening before the stock exchange halted trading in these receipts.

I apologize for this rather long road story, but there is a point to be made. When many investors reached stage three of those seven stages of grief, they let their anger get the better of them. Instead of accepting that bad things do just happen, they chose to pay someone else to take the installment receipts off their hands. Perhaps desperation played a role for some as well, but most of the institutional investors I knew were more angry than desperate.

Whether investors paid to get the receipts off their books or simply paid the second installment of $8, the ones who skipped right to stage six (reconstruction) were in a better place emotionally to focus on making back their losses. Anger is distracting and usually misplaced.

CHAPTER 15

SIGNS OF TROUBLE ON THE HORIZON, OR WHEN TO TAKE A DETOUR

There are many reasons to take a detour. Leaving Sturgis on my way to Minneapolis, Minnesota, I was perhaps 80 miles along the highway when I noticed I was near Badlands National Park. Many fellow riders told me that the Badlands were well worth visiting, so I promptly detoured to the loop through the park.

It didn't add more than an hour and half to my trip (with half an hour to stop several times and marvel at the cliffs, canyons, ravines, and hoodoos), but it was well worth the diversion. The sharply eroded buttes, pinnacles, and spires blend with the largest protected mixed grass prairie in the United States to paint a glorious picture. The Native American Lakota tribe named the area *mako sica*, meaning "land bad," which makes sense, since travel and all sorts of land uses are extremely difficult due to the steep slopes, loose dry soil, slick clay, and deep sand. The display is also very colourful: blue, black, grey (clay), and red (volcanic) rock make the badlands beautiful if uninhabitable.

Many detours are necessary that are far less enjoyable:

- You are lost.
- Something just doesn't feel right (or smells bad figuratively speaking).
- The way ahead is blocked.

In an earlier chapter, I suggested that the sensible thing people do when lost while driving is stop and look at a map or ask for directions (or if you're male, ask your wife to get directions). Investors are usually of two types: 1) those who will not stop, and 2) those who will stop but refuse to map a trail forward. The latter ones end the trip right there.

A good friend once recommended to me that "if you don't know what to do in the market, do nothing." If the maverick investor doesn't have an inkling of where we are in terms of the business cycle or losses keep mounting with every short-term trading decision, then it is wise to just *stop!* Before making any decisions, re-examine your objectives. Why did you take the route you did? Has anything really happened that would imply your current economic thinking is flawed, such as industry expectations being out of whack or your stock or fund selection no longer being suitable? If not, then get back on the road. If things have changed (war breaks out, a massive oil spill occurs, interest rates change direction unexpectedly), then get out that map and find another route.

If you simply have the heebie-jeebies, it may be wise to divest all stocks and bonds or mutual funds. Be careful to make sure it isn't panic that is motivating you. *Never panic!* Before doing anything as rash as cashing in all your chips, it's important to have first examined the circumstances rationally. You should be thinking, "I really don't know what to do, so I'll move to the sidelines," rather than, "Oh my God, I've got to save what dollars I have left!"

Those heebie-jeebies can often save your bacon. Sometime in the mid-'90s, I attended a group luncheon held by an investment firm that was promoting a company that sold magnets with astonishing financial results. As implausible as this might sound, it was a very compelling story at the time. Magnets are used to make electric motors and generators. Without these electric motors and generators, we would not have telephones, lights, electric heat, television, or computers. There are medical applications (e.g. magnetic resonance imaging, or MRI), as well as many others. The company insisted it would grow 30% to 35% indefinitely as the market for magnets kept growing, and since they sourced their supplies from down-and-out eastern Europe, the profit margins were generous.

I cannot explain it, but something "smelled bad" to me during that meeting with company management. It may have been the demeanour of the individuals or the "too good to be true" packaging. Nevertheless, I didn't buy into it.

In March of 1998, YBM Magnex International Inc. was still boasting of its plans to become "the world's leading producer of high-energy magnets." Six months later, the company was under investigation for laundering money for the Russian mafia and filed for bankruptcy protection. It was a hoax of mammoth proportions.

My case of the heebie-jeebies prevented a potentially grievous error in judgement. If something doesn't feel right, it's perfectly okay to detour around it and move on to make decisions that make sense both rationally and intuitively. Does this contradict what I said earlier about ignoring your instincts? *Intuition* is often used as a synonym for *instinct*, but I don't think that it is. I hate semantics, but I will provide my own definitions to clarify the distinction in my own mind:

> *Instinct* – a powerful impulse that feels natural rather than reasoned.

> *Intuition* – the ability to see clearly and intuitively into the nature of a complex person, situation, or subject.

Whether or not my definitions are literally correct isn't important to me. The point is that *instinctively*, when your bike begins to slip on an oil slick, you apply the breaks, and the result is an accident. *Intuitively*, you should keep the bike pointed straight ahead, maintain velocity, and try to keep it upright.

If you own a stock or bond in a company and it simply goes bust, or you have short-term paper in your portfolio and suddenly it isn't paying or stops trading (like billions of dollars of asset-backed commercial paper surely did not long ago), then you've hit a roadblock. How does one cope? You cope by remembering that it wasn't you, or your advisor, who created the roadblock. The way is blocked by things beyond your control. In most such cases, whether it's the Enron scandal or WorldCom (the telecommunications industry brainchild of Canadian-born convicted fraudster "Bernie" Ebbers), there's nothing to do but grin and bear it.

Step four of the seven stages of grief evokes feelings of depression, reflection, and a sense of isolation. Skip it. Millions of others got hoodwinked, so you certainly had lots of company, and the time spent mourning your loss (it's just money after all) would be better spent applying your newfound maverick know-how to finding a viable detour—one that gets you back on your investment track.

- If you are lost, stop everything and revisit your trail map. If you can't immediately identify a suitable detour, be prepared to get off the road and stay put until one becomes clear to you.
- If the road ahead is foggy and giving you the heebie-jeebies, take a detour.
- If the road is completely blocked, accept it and find another way to reach your objective.

The same good friend who suggested we do nothing if we don't know what we're doing also provided a tip that has proven to be especially insightful. He said, "If you don't have a sense of humour, then don't invest." A bit of levity occasionally provides the best solace following a financial disaster.

CHAPTER 16

LET IT RIDE?

OR SUCCESS CAN BE YOUR WORST ENEMY

Minneapolis is a nice clean city. People are friendly and the best word I can come up with to describe the population is *wholesome*. Electing to stay an extra day, I discovered that the legendary Dr. John was performing at a downtown jazz club and caught his show. A bit of New Orleans' funky rhythms in Minneapolis seemed like an opportunity I'd be a fool to pass up.

Confidence is an asset but also a potential liability. Very early in the morning before heading north towards Duluth and then across the border back into Canada, I wanted to take a photo of the city skyline. It seemed the best potential was at Boom Island Park on a tiny island in the historic Mississippi River, which runs through the Twin Cities of Minneapolis and St. Paul.

I parked on the grass and set up my camera, getting the best photo I could manage through the trees. Did I mention it was early in the morning? The grass was saturated with morning dew and therefore extremely dangerous for an 850-pound two-wheeler.

An experienced and confident rider (uh oh), I hopped on the bike, hit the throttle, and the next thing I knew, the bike and I are both down on the lawn like a couple of drunks after an open-bar wedding.

It seems that whenever I'm in this situation (alone with a bike down), it's always a woman who comes to my rescue. There's nothing wrong with this, mind you, it just seems odd, statistically speaking. Although I did spot a fellow on a bicycle and a lady jogger at the same time and called out, "Excuse me," the fellow completely ignored my plea. It was the lady who ran over to me and offered to help.

Together we set the bike upright. I thanked her and this time carefully drove the motorcycle over to the dry pavement. Am I not "man enough" to lift 850 pounds on my own? No, I'm not! I've tried a few times and just hurt myself, so now I don't even bother to try it alone.

Contrasted with the blistering hot winds I suffered riding the through prairies, cruising along the tree-lined highway north from Minneapolis was delightful. It was a comfortable 80°F (27°C) all the way from Duluth along the north coast of Lake Superior to the Grand Portage National Monument. This is where fur trappers of the North West Company (which eventually merged with the Hudson's Bay Company) would exchange furs for supplies before heading further west. By the way, when the trappers would run out of supplies, they would depend on the hospitality of natives for survival. History is riddled with examples of voyageurs or explorers blazing a trail into new lands, only to be followed by settlers who wiped out the native population that welcomed them.

The enthusiasm of Americans concerning their history is impressive. The fort was filled with employees demonstrating everything from crafting furniture out of lumber using antiquated hand tools to smoking fish over a smoldering fire, but there were also dozens of volunteers dressed in period costumes. Cool!

The border crossing back into Canada just before Thunder Bay, Ontario, was uneventful compared to my prior experience. The border guard mentioned he had already seen dozens of Sturgis rally T-shirts and waved me through without incident.

Confidence Can Be Your Worst Enemy

A common handicap with even seasoned professional investors is letting your ego get the better of you. When your stock picks or portfolio is performing extremely well, you begin to believe you're responsible.

In many ways, the success will be a byproduct of efforts to stick to a maverick investment discipline, but luck has an important role to play also.

A rising tide raises all ships, so if the market is generally going higher, so will your portfolio. A maverick investor will be capable of performing better than the market index employing even a few of the lessons outlined in this guidebook:

- Never panic.
- Avoid heavy traffic.
- Look for opportunities—the good ones never come to you.
- Focus on future rather than past performance.

- Accept mistakes and don't grieve or get angry—just move along.

While you are doing well, always keep in mind that it's also because the market is buoyant and helping your cause. Investors often get so caught up in their own success that they neglect to watch for the signs that the investment environment may change at any moment. (And there are many signs available, as we covered in earlier chapters.)

We've used a few companies as examples, so let's discuss a mutual fund I am very familiar with. This is the resource fund I launched and managed until departing the company I also launched and managed.

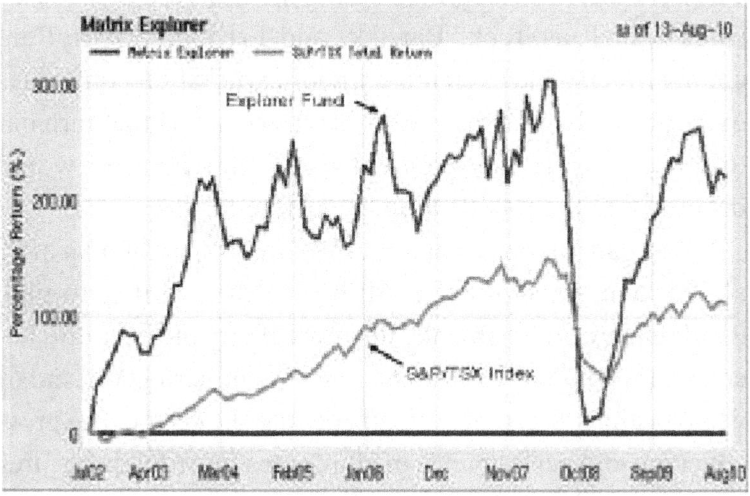

If investors had bought the fund close to its inception, they would have done extremely well for several years running despite a bumpy ride. (Now recall the advisor who suggested he'd never buy anything related to resource exploration stocks again.) The graph clearly illustrates why upside volatility is a not necessarily risky—maverick investors want return in excess of the overall market (in this case, the S&P/TSX Composite Index total return).

An early investor in the resource fund, having enjoyed good performance, would justifiably feel they had done a fine job of fund selection. As time went on, the press naturally caught onto the surge in global demand for resources. China's booming economy began to receive more publicity, and even the TV business news began posting updated prices of commodities such as gold, copper, nickel.

It is altogether likely (I've seen it first hand) that the same investor might buy into other resource funds as well. They might even begin dabbling in individual resource stocks, such as Teck, Barrick, and Freeport McMoRan, among others, and even more junior exploration companies quite probably. The more of these investments that turn out to be successful, the more convinced this investor would become that their skills are responsible for the success.

This can happen to anyone. We are all just human after all. As one grows more confident in their ability to pick good resource investments, the more likely the portfolio becomes less diversified. As the investment herd gets wind of what's happening, others stampede into the sector. The press coverage and performance of similar resource funds inspires the herd, which, of course, is causing stock prices to rise (demand being greater than supply). The better things get, the more vulnerable the investor is to letting their ego and confidence drown out all maverick intuition.

Rest assured that none of the strategists, investment gurus (who wrote books about resources long after the writing was on the wall), or research analysts was even considering the sector at the turn of the millennium. Resources had been underperforming and were largely ignored for almost two decades prior. It took one heck of a maverick to invest in such a fund in its early days.

A true maverick will grow increasingly suspicious when things are going too well. Just as I had to put my overconfidence in check after my bike and I went down, a maverick investor has to be ready at all times to question their own level of self-assuredness. The resource stocks were going up because demand for commodities was strong and the economies buying them were smoking hot. As you can see from the graph, once the financial crisis put a damper on global growth, it didn't matter whether or not you were a good picker of funds or stocks. Everything related to resources got crushed.

The more confident you are,
the more worried you should be.

The herd panicked and kept stampeding into cash equivalent investments (short-term securities, GICs, etc.) during late 2008 and most of 2009. You can also plainly see that there was an unprecedented opportunity to be a maverick early in 2009 and buy into those beat-up resource funds and stocks.

It's easy to see that taking profits along the way up, instead of doubling down, would work much better. Admittedly, hindsight is 20/20, but a bit of foresight can be precious.

My ride resumed after an evening's rest in Thunder Bay, Ontario. Lake Superior is notorious for its high winds, and the northern Ontario weather can be quite unpredictable. It was a chilly 60°F (16°C) in the morning with blistering winds all along the Trans-Canada Highway.

There's no better sign that I'm back in Canada than racing alongside a railway train going eastbound.

It's no coincidence that I chose the resource sector for the above example. I rode along the beautiful highway, catching glimpses of Lake Superior and its rugged shoreline and slowing down occasionally as trucks laden with freshly cut lumber got in my way. Signs of a rich mining heritage were scattered all along the route as well. I passed by the old Hemlo – David Bell Mine, now wholly owned by gold mining giant Barrick Gold. The Hemlo gold camp was first discovered in 1979 and opened in 1985. The Hemlo mines were originally estimated to hold 25 million ounces of gold and certainly rank as one of the biggest gold mines in Canada.

There were pockets of heavy rain on the way southeasterly, which is not much fun on a motorcycle. I was soon pooped out and stopped in Sault Ste. Marie for a much needed respite. The town is home to Essar Steel Algoma (formerly Algoma Steel) an integrated primary steel producer. Its products are sold in Canada and the United States, as well as overseas.

American entrepreneur Francis Clergue, who had settled in Sault Ste. Marie, founded Algoma Steel in 1902. However, times were tough for the steel industry during the post-9/11 recession, and Algoma Steel went bankrupt. After a substantial restructuring of the business, the company emerged from bankruptcy protection in 2004, and in April 2007, India's Essar Group purchased it.

The northern air was chilly again the next morning, but sunny, so I put on a sweater and my jacket and continued on my way along the north shore of Lake Huron. I've longed to ride this route for as long as I can remember but just never got around to touring the Great Lakes.

I passed the town of Bruce Mines, which was the first copper mining community ever in North America. Copper deposits at Bruce Mines were discovered by settlers in 1846, and mining began that same year. The mines were named after James Bruce, who was appointed the Governor General of Canada in 1846 as well. Thirty years later, the mines were closed due to floods and cave-ins. Although mining was restarted in 1915, by 1921, the mine was completely mothballed. The actual mine shaft is open to the public, but the town and vicinity depends on agriculture and tourism for sustenance nowadays.

I decided to cover a more modest distance that day and rolled into Sudbury to find a hotel. The city of Greater Sudbury is the largest community in northern Ontario. Sudbury began as a small lumber camp, but in 1883, during the construction of the Canadian Pacific Railway, the blasting and excavation revealled high concentrations of nickel and copper.

In the '30s, demand for nickel was so strong that Sudbury rebounded from the Great Depression far more quickly than other areas in North America. The fortunes of the city since then tend to ebb and flow with the demand and price of nickel.

For quite a long time, two companies, Inco and Falconbridge, dominated nickel mining in the prolific Sudbury Basin. Unfortunately, Brazilian mining giant Vale (formerly Companhia Vale do Rio Doce, or CVRD) now owns Inco and runs it under the name Vale Limited.

In a heated takeover battle, suitors wanting to buy

Falconbridge included Inco (prior to the Vale takeover), Phelps Dodge Corporation (which wanted to buy them both), and Xstrata plc. In the end, Xstrata won with a juicy all-cash offer, and Falconbridge became Xstrata Nickel.

Takeovers are another robust indicator of cycle tops and bottoms.

One of the best-kept secrets is that there is always a flurry of businesses taking over other businesses in cycle troughs and at cycle peaks. At low points in the economic cycle, premiums are not very big. The takeover price per share that one company offers to buy the other company is always higher, or at a *premium*, to where the share price was trading before the takeover bid was made. The acquiring company usually pays 15% to 20% above the market price when the economy and market are at a low point in the cycle. Whenever there are takeovers suddenly happening but with low premiums being paid, it's usually because companies can buy other companies cheaper than building or expanding their businesses in conventional ways. It's a sure sign the market is about to emerge from a trough, or low point, and will likely trend higher.

In contrast, takeover premiums during cycle peaks can be very generous, as much as 30% to 40% above the market price. Management teams are under extreme pressure to grow (often while organic growth in the industry is slowing) and their level of confidence has become excessive. Whenever there is a bunch of takeover attempts in one industry and the premiums are large, this usually means the industry is about to roll over and suffer hard times. If a takeover frenzy is occurring in a number of different industries at once, it's always a signal that the overall market is due for a correction. When companies pay such a ridiculously high price to purchase other companies, it's a sign that optimism and confidence have become contagious to the point of absurdity.

My own policy has always been to sell all shares in a company I own once the takeover announcement is made. There are numerous sophisticated arbitrage traders who bet big dollars to earn a few pennies buying and selling shares in companies being taken over or are "in play" between the day of the announcement and the closing of the transaction. My philosophy is that if I didn't own the shares before the takeover announcement, why would I buy them after the announcement? The potential returns playing the takeover game are skinny (unless you have millions of dollars to gamble with) compared to simply identifying and buying good investment candidates.

I apologize for getting off topic. I should probably have mentioned this takeover stuff earlier in the guidebook when discussing cycles and various indicators such as herd behaviour and press coverage, but, by golly, I didn't. It's better late than never, so give an old man a break and pardon the interruption. Now let's get back on topic and finish delving into the perils of letting success and overbearing confidence wreak havoc on your investment program.

Who hasn't bought a new car, new house, or other toys following a few good years at the office, factory, or warehouse? It's the natural thing to do. We feel successful and confident, so why not pamper ourselves? We do it even though deep down in our subconscious we are keenly aware that it may not be the smartest thing to do. We instinctively desire to better our circumstances, but intuitively we know that our good fortune could very well be short-lived.

In my opinion, it's certainly okay to go for it once in a while. After all, life is short. When it comes to managing your investment portfolio, however, it's best not to succumb to these same urges. I'll leave you with a couple of tips:

- When the performance of your portfolio and your level of confidence are soaring, become more conservative and wary.
- If you and everyone else you know lacks any confidence at all, get busy.

THE FINAL CHAPTER

TRAIL'S END

Just before I ride the last leg of my bike tour, I feel compelled to reflect on whether I've satisfied my five-point plan:

1) Decide where you want to go.
2) Map out a way to go in order to get there.
3) Always be prepared to adjust your route due to obstructions and detours.
4) Getting to your destination is your only measure of success.
5) Enjoy the ride.

I wanted to travel through America's heartland and experience first-hand riding the legendary Pacific Coastal Highway and to visit the wild and crazy Sturgis rally for my first time on my way back. I carefully planned a route that would balance a desire to get where I wanted to go within a timeframe that seemed reasonable (one month) but also allowed me to explore some beautiful country.

Upon reflection, there were some obstacles: road construction and hot weather occasionally got in the way of my planned route, but I avoided panic by discovering patience, and the odd detour kept me on the straight and narrow. As a bonus, I managed to detour north from Minnesota and finally ride along the northern coast of the Great Lakes.

I got where I wanted to go successfully, and boy did I ever enjoy the ride.

It takes a concerted effort and a bit of good luck to be successful at whatever one does. This maverick investor's guidebook may help you focus your effort on the important things:

- You won't make the same mistakes as the uninitiated would, because you know what a maverick investor *won't do*.
- What you *will do* is invest your savings successfully and in a consistent and *measured* fashion.

- You will have your own collection of "road stories" to learn from, and perhaps you'll share them with novice investors, helping to steer them clear of financial disasters and towards prosperity.
- Whether your objective is to grow your money so that you can buy a new boat or home, or simply to have a few bucks when you retire, you will successfully get there and know you've *enjoyed the ride*.

The maverick mindset will help you make better decisions in many situations. Why buy a house during a real estate boom? A home is often the single biggest investment a family will ever make. Be patient and begin shopping for your new home when there are plenty of sellers and very few buyers.

If the economy is relatively strong and interest rates seem high, choose a variable rate mortgage and wait until they fall before locking the mortgage in at a fixed rate. If you've heeded the above advice about buying real estate low, chances are good rates will be low at the same time. So instead of foolishly expecting them to decline below zero, go ahead and lock in a reasonable fixed rate for as long as the bank will let you.

Have you ever hopped in the car to drive twenty miles to buy an item on sale for $5 cheaper than the local offering? Have you ever factored in the cost of the gasoline and your time beforehand? A bit of financial analysis goes a long way towards making wiser decisions.

The last leg of my road trip was both a relief (to be going home) and a bit disappointing (I wanted to just keep on riding). I decided to follow old Highway 69 straight south from Sudbury until it hooked up with Highway 400 south past Barrie to Toronto. It was a perfect day—not too hot or too cold— and it was a smooth ride home thanks to so much road construction of late (government spending to create jobs following such a long economic slump).

As I lurk around the house, reminiscing about the trip—thinking about where I've been and visualizing the remarkable scenery I'd seen—I can't help but also revisit some key points addressed in this guidebook:

There is no single measure of success.

Increasing your wealth some, a bunch, or a whole lot will depend on how much effort you're willing to put into it. If you are satisfied with your effort, and you have reasonable expectations based on your effort, then you will be successful.

The stock price of a company goes up because people are buying it.

In fact, the price of anything goes up because there are more buyers than sellers. Understanding this dynamic will go a long way to improving your investment results.

Minimum risk occurs when perceived risk is at a maximum.

Most investors, the press, and the academic community misunderstand investment risk.

Rely on your own judgement and not the opinions of others.

Other people are motivated by other things; only you can

make decisions consistent with your objectives and tolerance for taking risks.

If your bets aren't working, stop betting.

The best thing to do when confused and making bad decisions is to stop and do some thinking. Be rational, not emotional.

Myth: Diversification reduces risk.

Unless you diversify efficiently, attempts to diversify can reduce returns and actually increase volatility.

Myth: Buy and hold works.

When the environment around you changes fast and furiously, you must be prepared to rapidly exploit new opportunities or be left in the dust.

A great track record might actually guarantee poor performance.

Only future performance matters. There has never been evidence to suggest good investment performance in the past can be repeated.

Don't fall in love with your ideas.

Be careful not to let *investing* deteriorate into *gambling*.

Timing is everything.

It is extremely difficult to do everything at just the right time. It is quite profitable to do most things at a good time but dangerous to do many things at the wrong time.

Don't blame the guide.

Bad things happen because of outside influences. Pointing an accusing finger at yourself or your financial advisor is just a waste of energy—energy better spent fixing the problem.

You need to know where you are before you can know where to go.

This is so obvious to me that it hardly requires further comment.

The more confident you are, the more worried you should be.

Investing is all about managing uncertainty. Once you feel certain about everything, what is it you think you're managing?

Welcome to the trail, fellow maverick!